It's A Matter of Perspective

Nuggets of Encouragement for the Journey

CHERYL TILGHMAN

Published by Cheryl Tilghman
Graphic design by Karen Bowlding
Cover photo by Lilkar

ISBN: 978-0-578-82300-3

Printed in the United States

Acknowledgements

This book is dedicated to my four children Tiffany, Tasha, Tracy, and Michael II. I am so proud of who they have become as adults. God had gifted each one with love, compassion, humor, intelligence, and creativity. They have encouraged and inspired me to be my very, best and to live life to the fullest during my parenting journey. God's grace and faithfulness has allowed me to be here to see them as self-sufficient adults with successful careers and family. I thank God for giving me these four special blessings and an opportunity of being their mother. They are an integral part of my spiritual journey. Without my children, and the many challenges involved in the turns of events in my life, I would not have been able to share the stories and nuggets of information contained in this book. God is the joy and the strength of my life and He does all things well! To God be the glory!

Contents

It's A Matter of Perspective

Our perspective is formed by the totality of our personal lifespan of events. It is a reflection of the way we think, speak and act. Whether good, bad, or mediocre, life's experiences uniquely affect individuals differently. It's not uncommon for two or more persons to have, what seems to be the same experience, at the same time, yet when describing the experience, each person expresses a different account of the event. The various experiences we have endured or enjoyed, "frame" our perspectives. Our perspectives have the potential of keeping us stagnant, and unfruitful, or propelling us into making positive changes, and becoming fruitful.

Changing our perspective entails making a conscious decision for mindset and lifestyle changes. It's truly a personal decision to be fruitful or unfruitful. However, once the decision to be fruitful is made, it is important to focus on the desired results and eliminate distractions. Negative attitudes do not develop overnight, so prepare to do some self-care work to nurture and cultivate a positive attitude and a healthy perspective. Be patient during the process. Although some of life's occurrences can be disheartening, how one chooses to think about those occurrences is important to changing their perspective.

The negative blows in life can be softened by scheduling specific times within each day, week and month that are filled with enjoyable activities and positive interactions. Fill your time with things that make you smile such as, uplifting media conversations, exercise classes, fun events, time with encouraging friends, relaxing, and meditating on God's Word. Other ways to enjoy enriching experiences are participating in character building activities, attending self-help classes and motivational conferences. It is also a great idea to read nourishing, fictional and nonfictional books. The aforementioned activities help to fill the mind, heart and spirit with pleasure, wisdom, and knowledge. They also build confidence, character, and stability.

God encourages Christians to renew their minds by reading the Bible and meditating on it day and night. One undeniable truth is that burying the Word of God deep down in man's spirit will produce outcomes that yield favorable results. Loving God, reading his word, fasting, and praying, altogether assist Christians in reaching the destiny God desires for each life. God's Word states, "to be like trees planted by the water; not easily moved." (Jeremiah 17:8) The purpose is to develop unshakeable faith and move in the power of God available to all Christian believers. The word of God admonishes and encourages followers of Christ with this truth, "I can do all things through Christ who strengthens me." (Philippians 4:13)

Positive mindsets are a part of a larger plan which includes learning new ways of thinking and doing things. God, in his infinite wisdom and power, could have created the world in a moment, in an hour, or in just one day. However, he decided it best, to create the world in six days, and rest on the seventh day. God shows his children that resting is important. We must rest after the completion of any assignment, job or project, before moving on to another.

God's example of working with an organized thought process, shows us how to accomplish tasks in decency and in order. He is the Master Creator, King of Kings and Lord of Lords! His master plan is for His children's good, and His glory. As we travel in this journey called life, changing our perspectives to line up with God's mindset, will assure our arrival at the right place, at the right time for an amazingly, abundant destiny!

The Caterpillar Transforms Into A Butterfly

The butterfly is one of my favorite insects! Its transformation process, as well as its beautiful colors, capture my interests. When I saw the process of how a caterpillar transitioned into a butterfly, I was troubled at first, by what it had to endure, before transforming into the fullness of its destiny. I soon found out the importance and necessity of the struggle the butterfly experiences while getting free from the cocoon. Getting out of the cocoon is an integral part of the butterfly's transformation process. The struggle helps to strengthen the butterfly's wings, so that it will be able to fly, after it escapes from its resistant protective covering.

It starts out as a caterpillar, all green or black and fuzzy with a bunch of legs used to crawl on the ground. Within a short period of time, it changes into a cocoon. A short time later, it transforms into a beautiful butterfly. It breaks out with force and boldly starts flying everywhere. No longer a slow, creepy, crawling, struggling insect. Now, a beautiful insect with grace, tenacity and speed! No longer bound by the baggage of the body of its past, rather now, with a beautifully, colored body and the marvelous freedom to fly everywhere!

Some people gave their lives to Christ but didn't receive the essential follow up care needed to become a mature Christian. Although now a part of the Christian family, they were not given the spiritual tools to be an effective member. They don't know they need to hear the Word of God for their faith to grow, so they infrequently attend church services and Bible study classes. "So then faith comes by hearing, and hearing by the word of God." (Romans 10:17) When we're not diligent at reading God's Word, and not paying attention to His voice, we may miss the many things God uses to send blessings and to teach valuable life lessons. This is one of the reasons why many are crawling through life with no knowledge of their purpose or the necessary information to pursue it.

Life is full of distractions and we fall prey to its pitfalls. This is what most refer to as the struggle. We can liken it to the butterfly's experience because it is similar to what the butterfly experiences in its transformation process. The struggle, which builds character, power, strength, and tenacity, is necessary for the transformation to be completed. If the butterfly was not experiencing all of what it needed for its transformation, it would not be the beautiful insect it becomes after undergoing its process. We need all of our life's experiences to get us from where we started out in life, to our place of destiny. God's plan includes transforming us to be the greatest encouraging, empowering, impactful blessing we can be, in the lives of others.

Looking at the beauty of the butterfly's transformation process, provides hope that we can make it through anything God allows us to go through. He never gives us more than we can individually bare. He will always be there assisting us, with the grace and mercy we need, to get through our process. We only need to ask, with a pure heart, which means, without manipulation or ill intent. After we have been through life's fiery trials, it is then, that we have successfully completed the process and are ready to be who God has fashioned us to be.

For many years, I struggled, but didn't understand why I had to go through all of what I did. I kept being told that God doesn't waste any of the things we experience in life, whether good or bad. He allows us to go through these things, for His glory. We are God's workmanship. He knows how He created us, and He promised that He would not give us more than we can individually bare. God has graced me to go through a multitude of life's struggling experiences. With His help, I have made it through those processes, and I am still standing strong! God said He would never leave nor forsake his children. He is always there, no matter what is going on in life. God is no respecter of persons. What He makes happen for one, He will do for another.

Don't curse life's struggle with your mouth. Life and death are in the power of the tongue. Speak life! God is worthy! God deserves to be honored, adored, loved and worshipped. It is our pleasure to walk in the light of His presence and serve Him. Basking in the presence of God allows us to experience the peace that passes all understanding, as we meditate on the truths of God's Word. He is faithful and His promises are true! God will see us through!

Here Today & Memories

The death, of any living thing, sends the lover of the thing, into a process. The grief process entails questioning, feelings of guilt and blaming, and eventually healing. One never forgets the person or thing that died. The memories are carried deep within the heart and mind forever. The process can be very challenging and self-reflecting; however, when one comes out of the process, the heart and the mind typically views the situation with a new perspective.

When my mother transitioned in 2011, it was hard for me to believe she was not going to be here for me to see or interact with anymore. She was 85 years old and had greatly suffered the week before she transitioned from this life to eternity. To get past the grief, I reasoned with myself that she had lived a long, full life and she was not suffering anymore. The Bible teaches us, "to be absent from the body is to be present with the Lord. (2 Corinthians 5:8) Mentally I understood the teaching, but my heart was hurting from her absence. I held on to what I could hold dear to my heart. It was the memories of who she was, and the many times we spent together. Good memories, sad memories, fun memories, as well as angry memories. Most of all, humorous memories, that my family and I still share, whenever we gather to celebrate holidays and other family occasions.

Think of what a blessing it is to share memorable times with loved ones. Isn't it great spending time loving, laughing, playing, hugging, nurturing and serving each other? Do you have memories of the times spent working together as a team? What about the memories of accomplishing goals and conquering challenging situations? Special memories create the warm and fuzzy feelings of belonging and unity that are important in a family. When a loved one transitions from life to eternity, family memories help us to appreciate each other more. We realize that we are all on this journey through life. We will have to leave this earthen vessel, at some point, to obtain God's promise of everlasting life. It is important to create special memories that will continue to live on in the hearts, minds and spirits of those who have to continue living the journey. Families cherish memories like these most at times of transition. They look back and realize that the time spent gathering was special. It was one of the puzzle pieces in building the family legacy.

"Til Death Do Us Part" – Growing God's Family

Marriage is a lifetime, covenant gift from God. It is designed to assist two imperfect individuals, a man and a woman, in becoming one flesh, in the eyesight of God. Marriage embodies all of the fruit of the Spirit; love, joy, peace, patience, kindness, goodness, faithfulness, gentleness and self-control. (Galatians 5:22) The Marriage covenant requires the partners to love one another for the rest of their natural lives. God's definition of love is, "Love is patient, love is kind. It does not envy, it does not boast, it is not proud. It does not dishonor others, it is not self-seeking, it is not easily angered, it keeps no record of wrongs. Love does not delight in evil but rejoices with the truth. It always protects, always trusts, always hopes, always perseveres. Love never fails." (1 Corinthians 13:4-8a)

Most find loving one person in all of these ways for the rest of their natural life, a challenge. Accomplishing the "becoming one" takes a lot of work, but is doable, when God is in it. God requests the couple to be fruitful and multiply, to grow His family. As with all Christians, they should use their gifts and unique talents for building up the Kingdom of God. God's idea for marriage is, to display His unconditional love, for everyone, and to be a representation of His love for His Bride, the church. Marriage is typically only successfully demonstrated, when the fruit of Love is evident and fully matured, through the love of God and the fellowship of the sweet Holy Spirit. Successful marriages require sacrificial love, shown by acts of forgiveness, endurance, and tenacity. Each spouse has a responsibility to be selfless; dying to their own desires for the good of the marriage. A selfless attitude and behavior models true sacrificial love. God's grace and mercy helps spouses to love each other without harboring bitterness, resentfulness and unforgiveness.

God so loved the world that He gave His only son, Jesus, to die and be raised from the dead. (John 3:16) The blood Jesus shed in His death and resurrection, covers past, present and future believers. All baptized believers are freed from the original sin, caused by the disobedience of Adam and Eve, and have the opportunity of experiencing an amazing, direct, intimate relationship with God in the Trinity. The Trinity is God the Father, Jesus His Son and the sweet Holy Spirit. What an incredible way God chose to show that He loves us! God endured the loneliness of being without His son Jesus, while He watched Jesus be abused and crucified as the sacrificial lamb, for the purpose of securing the gift of salvation for His "Bride," the Body of Christ!

In the Bible, God affectionately shares about how much He loves his "Bride." When God makes the divine connection between a man and a woman, he has already decided on their Kingdom purpose. Their main focus should be in the things they can do to help with the building up of the Kingdom of God. Married couples are called to be a representation of God's love for His Bride. His grace and mercy are fresh and new every morning, which allows us to start over every day, with a newness of life and purpose. Those who have not yet found their mate, but are destined for the gift of marriage, are waiting patiently in expectation, while in preparation for the purpose and call God has placed on their lives.

They are readying themselves to fulfill God's assigned plans. The Bible teaches us that marriage and family are God's idea. He is modeling His love for His Bride, as well as positioning them for growing His Christian family on earth. God's idea is that marriage is for a lifetime. There are situations that harden the heart of the spouses towards each other, in such a way, that the couple will divorce. Sometimes it's to prevent harm, hurt or danger to each other, and their children.

God's idea was, and still is the best; however, many of us are still growing in our knowledge and understanding of God and His plans for our lives. We end up having to go through multiple tribulations, before asking for God's forgiveness, and beginning the diligent work of repentance. True repentance is discontinuing sinful actions, thoughts, or words, accepting the truth of God's word, then taking the necessary steps to walk in it.

Divorce is the death of a marriage. God declared in marriage, the two become one flesh. Divorce tears the one flesh apart. It wreaks havoc in the lives of the spouses and children of the union, whether biological or blended. Fortunately, some couples, on the brink of divorce, choose to salvage the marriage. They experience restoration, after they decide to keep their covenant, and to do the challenging work discussed, in intense counseling sessions. They breakthrough stronger, better and wiser with desire, ability, and a wealth of information and knowledge. They pour into other couples, on the brink of divorce, and have a desire, to grow, to heal, and to continue, in their marriage covenants. Only God can work that kind of miracle, to demonstrate to His people, that true love can endure all things!

The enemy to our soul, most call the spirit Satan, comes as an angel of light. Unfortunately, his goal is to steal, kill and destroy, breaking down loving marriages, strong family units, and fortified relationships. He especially hates marriages where the two have endured many tests and trials and are walking in victory. The enemy works overtime at creating confusion, for fortified relationships and tearing down the Christian family structure. He does not want spiritually strong people to be on one accord. Faith-filled, fortified believers have the ability to tear down the kingdom of darkness that Satan is working hard to build.

When we put the Bible's teachings into the proper perspective, we realize the life we are graced to live is not about us individually. It is about the work God wants to do through his family of believers. We are His ears, eyes, feet, hands and mouth. We are the ones who need to do the work, to further His Kingdom on earth. Each one, reach one, and build God's family of believers.

Suddenly Does Happen!

God is an awesome God! Nothing is impossible with Him! God has shown His love for me in many supernatural, suddenly, ways! As a single parent of four, stair-step children, my salary alone wasn't enough to make ends meet. Yet, through it all, God showed me His loving care, by making a way out of no way! I'm sharing with you some of the ways God gently helped me to believe that suddenly does happen!

One of those times is when we needed toothpaste and I didn't have enough money to purchase it. I prayed to God and asked Him to help me afford the toothpaste. I went to the store, by faith, thinking it could be on sale. As I was going into the store through the revolving door, I looked down on the ground and there was a coupon for a dollar off of a national brand of toothpaste! I was overjoyed by the discovery! When I got to the toothpaste aisle, I was amazed that the toothpaste was on sale! I was able to purchase the toothpaste with the coupon and only had to pay a few cents for the tax! I went all the way home praising God for His faithfulness and goodness!

Many times, He has kept me from getting into serious car accidents. One time, in particular, I was driving, and my mother and I were leaving a gas station. I was close to the mouth of the exit, when a car came speeding down the street. Suddenly, the car turned up into the mouth of the gas station exit, to avoid hitting the car in front of it. The car had stopped for the traffic light. When the car turned up into the mouth of the gas station, in an instant, that car and my car almost had a head on collision. There must have been an angel between us that stopped the impact. My mother was in shock and awe of what had happened. The Lord kept me at perfect peace during this dangerous event allowing me to calm my mother.

Several times I have been on the beltway, and I know it was the angels moving me along or slowing me down. I was too tired to be driving and there were cars that were blocked when they tried to run me off the road. Once I was traveling too fast, and a car was coming off of the ramp too slowly, and I couldn't get my car to slow down fast enough. I had pushed the brake pedal down to the floor. Angels must have intervened, while I was calling on the name of Jesus anticipating an impact. But God stopped my car from impacting with the other car, and all of the cars behind me were able to slow down appropriately. No accidents resulted in the incident. Hallelujah to our risen King!

My first house had three bedrooms and one bathroom. Although I was upset when the tub drain was clogged, I took it in stride. I spent several days using unclogging drain solutions, and plunging, yet nothing worked. I could not afford a plumber. When I was fed up with all of my attempts to unclog the drain, I got an idea. I had been attending an intercessory prayer meeting once a week, and I was growing spiritually by reading the Bible, praying, praising and worshipping God. I was also learning how to use the Word of God to solve problems. The past several days I had been plunging with all of my might, with no favorable results. So, when I approached the tub this day, I decided to plunge while praying. I started calling on the name of Jesus and fiercely plunging. I started declaring and decreeing that the drain clog release and clear, in the name of Jesus. I was also reciting the promises of God that He said He would supply all of our needs according to His riches in glory. At that moment, I needed my drain unclogged. I continued plunging with force for a few minutes calling on the name of Jesus. Suddenly, the clog released, and all of the water in the tub started going down the drain. I couldn't help but praise Him! Hallelujah! Faith, with elbow grease, got the job done!

He Is A Waymaker!

I left Ipswich, England as a domestic violence survivor and a single parent of four children, ages four to eight. My sister was gracious and allowed the five of us to stay with her family in their one-bedroom apartment. Eight of us in a one-bedroom apartment was challenging; however, I was grateful for the blessing of a place to stay, to get back on my feet. Things were extremely tight financially. I had a little money I had saved, while working on the Air Force Base in England, but it wasn't enough to start a new life in Maryland. I immediately contacted my previous supervisor at the government office I had resigned from when I went to England. Personnel called to let me know they definitely wanted me back. They needed a person with my experience, but I would have to wait for human resources to complete the steps necessary for a rehire.

While I was waiting on the human resource department at the federal government job, I had a dream. I dreamt, very clearly, that I was in an office building. I was being asked to go from one location in the building to another by different people. I felt very comfortable there and I knew where to go without getting directions from other employees. I could see the areas very clearly labeled and I was going without assistance from those who were working there. I didn't know what the dream meant, so I continued to wait on the federal government to respond to me about the job because human resources had promised me a position.

Government paperwork takes a while to process. I didn't start the federal government job until eight weeks after I had contacted them. Directly after accepting the federal government job, my cousin's wife came to me with an application for a job with her quasi-government agency. With no hesitation, I submitted the application. The job description fit my skill sets perfectly. The annual salary was more than what I was slated to make at the federal government job I had already accepted. The position also offered a great opportunity for career advancement.

The same week I started the federal government job, I got a call from the quasi-government job, requesting I come in for an interview. When I went for the interview, I recognized the location as the building I had seen in my dream. It was a déjà vu moment. The environment and surroundings were exactly as I had seen in my dream. There were two managers needing a position filled, so both were present for my interview. I felt I had represented myself well. It was evident at the end of the interview that I was a highly qualified candidate for either position. On the way home from the interview, I had a peace in my spirit that I had already gotten the job.

Three weeks after the interview, I got a call offering me one of the positions. HR didn't tell me which position, but it didn't matter to me at that point. All I cared about at the time was first, the significant increase in salary, second, an opportunity for career growth and third, the other benefits available to afford a better life for my four children and myself. It didn't take long for me to decide to take the leap of a lifetime. I submitted a two week notice to resign from the federal government. Then, I confidently walked through the doors of my employment opportunity and eagerly started my new career with the quasi-government.

I was making a little over $16,000 with my new career. I desperately wanted to move my family from my sister's crowded one-bedroom apartment. We needed to have a place of our own to call home. However, I did not financially qualify for a three - bedroom apartment in my sister's complex or anywhere else in the area. God was in control of the situation. Although I didn't qualify financially,

I was given a three-bedroom apartment, based on my good credit.

There were a lot of challenges living in the apartment. Maintenance workers were coming into my apartment during the day leaving my door unlocked when they left. They had been watching TV and eating my children's snacks. The neighbors downstairs would blast their music so loud, on the weekend, that the neighbors above me were knocking on my door asking me to turn down the music, until they realized it was the apartment below me. Also, the neighbors above me would take baths with the water so high in the tub that the water would run down into my apartment wetting up my bathroom ceiling. After a few months of this occurring, I was forced into using an umbrella in the bathroom so that the water would not run down from the ceiling, while my children or I were in there. When the ceiling became saturated with the water, it started sagging so low, I had to call the rental office to get them to take it down, so that it wouldn't fall on us. The exposed wood from the floorboards was the only thing left of the bathroom ceiling and we really had to carry the umbrella every time to protect us from the drainage upstairs. Although I had spoken to these neighbors and the rental office, the occurrences continued to happen.

Just before I moved from the apartment, I called the health department to report the issues with the bathroom ceiling. The call brought urgency to the situation and the issue was fixed expeditiously.

We had been living in the apartment for a year. I was fed up with apartment living. I spoke to one of my uncles about the many negative experiences my children, and I, had to endure and my desire to own a home. Without hesitation, he told me to find a home I could afford, and he would give me a financial gift equal to the down payment amount to purchase it.

I found a real estate agent and was introduced to the house my children and I would soon call home. When we pulled up, I was enamored by the cute little doll house look on the outside. It was a thirty year old Cape Cod, single family house, with a large shade tree out front. It had a separate driveway to the right of the house, and a walkway from the street that ended with four steps leading up to the front door. It had white stucco siding with red shutters and a red door. When walking through the front door, the baby blue, plush carpet, and baby blue walls trimmed with white borders, immediately grabbed my attention. My favorite color is blue, so it captured my heart.

When I went upstairs to the one large bedroom, I thought about the three little bears, and I pictured my three daughters, in that room, side by side. My son and I would be across the hall from each other on the main floor. The basement was a great place for my children to play indoors, and the backyard, with large pine shade trees, was a nice size for the children to play outdoors. It was also enticing for cookouts and other fun activities. I fell in love with the house and could see myself and my children there for a long time.

The house was affordable, but during our visit, I had seen one issue that was concerning. It was one of the walls in the basement. It seemed to be bulging a little. The family had used fresh paint throughout and in the basement area, so the wall was just a little noticeable. But when I heard why the family needed to move, my heart went out to their situation. The Veteran had major lung and breathing issues and was on oxygen. He and his wife and children needed to move to Arizona to a drier climate to preserve his life. The doctors had told the family a drier climate would give him a better quality of life ultimately helping to extend his life. I made the decision to purchase the home with the veteran's Assumable Veteran's loan based on the family's need to move, and the fact that my mortgage payment would be less than my apartment rent. Also, my utilities would be reasonable because I was eligible to take advantage of the gas, electric and water company's budget plans. I felt it was the perfect home for me and my children at that time. I had determined we would be there about five years. It was a good decision and many fun memories were created during the early years of home ownership!

However, as the years progressed, our home needed many repairs. One of the main issues plaguing the house was the water that seeped into the basement everytime a hard rain fell. It was coming in through the same wall I was concerned about during the first viewing of the house. One of my next-door neighbors had an in-ground pool that he would empty out into his yard. The reservoir of water would sit in the yard below the surface. When it rained, the ground could not hold any more water, so it started coming into my basement wall. It also seeped into the floor on the left side of the basement. It was so bad, at one time, when I went down into the basement, that the water was up to my knees. The drain, that should have been on the floor in the basement, was cemented shut, so there was no way to drain the water out. I was struggling to get the basement drained each time. I felt like I was between a rock and a hard place.

Then, one of my neighbors became an angel blessing to me and my children. He would come over to my house and use my wet and dry vacuum to suck the water up, then take it up the stairs, and throw it out the back door to the backyard. It was a huge task to empty out the whole basement of water, up to my knees. Although the basement flooded frequently, he would come over with a smile and drain it for me. He never complained. He never asked for a dime. I was so grateful! He knew I was unable to pay him. I was struggling to make my monthly payments and I wasn't getting child support payments, at that time. God knew I was going to have that problem and allowed my neighbor to be willing, and able, to assist me in getting this major job done. Eventually, I refinanced the house and was able to get the money to have a French drain and a sump pump put in. It was a long time coming, but what a relief it was when the job was completed!

Since the house was over 30 years old, it had a lot of problems needing to be fixed. The house became a money pit. I was unable to keep up with the home repairs, credit bills, along with affording the many other expenses of my growing children. When I moved into the house, I was receiving child support payments. But, a couple of years later, the payments ceased.

Eventually, I was behind two months with my mortgage, and I was moving towards foreclosure. I was going backwards fast. But God... God orchestrated a way for me to move into a Section 8 townhouse to take the pending foreclosure pressure off of me. Although they were only giving me fifty dollars a month to help make the ends meet, I only had to pay one utility bill per month and that was a big savings from the single-family house expenses.

We lived in the Section 8 townhouse for four years. Living there helped me to regroup and get my financial footing. I was also getting financial increases from my quasi-government job. After two years, the section 8 management office told me I would have to pay market rent since my salary superseded their financial scale. They told me I was now able to purchase a home. My children were just starting college and I wasn't sure I wanted to take on the responsibility of purchasing a new home. But God told me I was living in a home that would benefit another family like it did for me, at the time I needed it. If I stayed there, I was keeping the other family's blessing. So, I set out to purchase another home. Needless to say, God provided the new home!

I had lost two new cars due to the oil running out of the cars immediately after oil changes, causing the engines to go bad. I had been taking the cars to car repair shops that charged a cheaper price for oil changes than the dealer; however, in the scheme of things, I paid the price of having to get two new cars, because I wanted to save money on the oil changes. I really needed a car to get around with four young children. After the second car engine failed, I ended up going to a "Slasher" car sale at a large car dealership. It was a cloudy, balmy day. There were several interested buyers at the sale and excitement was brewing. The goal was to look over the used cars, and choose the one you wanted, and sit in it.

The price was already posted on the car, but the purchaser had the opportunity to make a deal, with the salesman, to get the best deal. The first car I saw, that I wanted, was a green minivan with a beige interior. Several others were interested in the same car, so we all were able to sit in it. When the salesman came over, the person who got in first had the opportunity to purchase it at the slashed price, but if they decided they didn't want it, the next person could get it and so on. The first person decided to purchase, so I had to choose another car.

I walked around the lot and found a blue, Buick LeSabre Sedan with a blue interior. It had 116,000 miles. Buicks had a reputation of lasting well over 116,000 miles, so I wasn't concerned about the mileage. The body of the car, and the interior looked really good. One major issue with the car was the roof of the car was smashed in like a large boulder had fallen on it. Although it had this major flaw, I decided it was the best option for me, if the price was right. I sat in the car and waited for the salesman to come over. The original price was $4,800. The slashed price was $2,500, so I accepted the deal. After the financing was completed, my monthly note was only $98.00! The salesman also agreed to have the roof fixed, so that after the fix, the car looked like it was brand new! I bought the car in Virginia but since I lived in Maryland, I had to have the car inspected in Maryland. The inspection revealed a little rust on the exhaust system, so the dealership had to replace the whole exhaust system, before the car could pass the Maryland inspection. The car was a true blessing and served me well. Within a couple of years, I was able to purchase a brand-new car.

It was the morning after a snowstorm. The temperature was high enough above freezing for the snow to start melting. I was teaching at a local elementary school and there was a two-hour delayed arrival for students and teachers that day. When I arrived at school, I parked on the soft shoulder, near the driveway, at the edge of the school property where there was still a few mounds of snow and mud. When I came out to leave for the day, the snow under the wheels of my car had melted and there was just a little grass but mostly mud. I got into my car and attempted to pull off, but the wheels of the car kept spinning. My car was stuck in the mud. I tried everything I knew, but it was to no avail. As I got out of the car to assess what to do, a large, burly man with a beard was walking up the driveway. He seemed to have come out of nowhere and asked if he could help. I yielded and allowed him to get inside of my car and take the wheel. The man tried multiple times to rock back and forth and change the wheel positions. The wheels continued to spin as he stepped on the gas. He still couldn't get the traction necessary to get the car moved. When I looked up, another man appeared from in front of the car. He had noticed us trying to free the car and started walking toward us. He stood and watched, but he didn't say anything. He just started to assist the man behind the wheel. No matter what strategies were used, they couldn't get the car out. Shortly thereafter, a third man joined. He started pushing the front of the car and working in concert with the other man who was pushing to free the car. As they were pushing, the wheel began to spin so fast that the man on the left front side of the car was splattered with thick mud, from his head to his feet. I stood there apologizing, but neither man said a word to me. All three men were completely focused on getting the car out of the mess. The spinning tires splashed mud all over the hood, doors and windows of the car. Despite the mess, the men worked tirelessly to free the car and release themselves from this uncanny dilemma. Up until this point, I hadn't thought to pray. I started praying and asking God to help them come up with a strategy to get my car out of the mud mess. Alas, an ideal strategy was used. One of the two men saw a piece of cardboard box on the side of the lot. He placed the cardboard under the front wheels to get traction. It worked! The man in my driving seat was able to get the car out of the mud and move it onto the surface of the driveway. When the driver got out of the car, I graciously thanked him. He proceeded on his way back down the driveway where I first saw him approaching me. The man covered in mud, took the remaining snow off of the side of the curb and used it to wash off the mud on his face, arms and clothes. I stood there while apologizing over and over for the mess, but he didn't look at me nor did he say anything either. The third man turned and walked to his car without looking at me or saying anything either. I immediately thought about the Biblical story of Shadrach, Meshach, and Abednego in the fiery furnace as told in Daniel 3:26. They were not in the furnace by themselves and neither were those three men. I was praying during the incident that God would give them strategies to free my car. God made a way out of no way by bringing together four strangers. I did not know the three men who came to help me. They were not concerned about getting dirty or what would happen to them. They were only focused on what needed to be done and how they were going to accomplish the task. I didn't have anything to give them, and they didn't seem to care. They were successful at the mission they accepted by helping me, the damsel in distress. Anytime, anywhere, and anyhow, He is an amazing waymaker!

Opinions vs Truth

Christianity starts in the heart of a person. Proverbs 21:2. "A person may think their own ways are right, but the Lord weighs the heart." God looks at (judges) the heart (motives, intentions) of a person. Salvation is a heart decision. On the outside, all may seem well, but the posture of the heart is viewed and taken into consideration when God decides what He is going to do. He knows our past, present and future. We must come to God our Father as a little child, with pure intentions and motives, submitted to His Lordship as Father, to be the greatest in the kingdom of Heaven. Matthew 18:2-5

We are responsible, and will be held accountable, for what we know but do not act on. It is sin for us, if we know better but choose to do otherwise. We must repent daily for the sins we commit by commission and omission. We have a loving Father, who only wants the best for His children. He wants us to have life and have it more abundantly. The Word of God is life. Choose Life!

All Things Are Possible If You Believe

God has done so many amazing things in my life! He is always a present help in the time of trouble. I can always depend on Him to help me work through every situation or circumstance that presents itself in my life. Although I grew up in the church, I wasn't living my life for the Lord. I knew the basics of the Christian life, but didn't know about a personal relationship with Jesus. When I came into the knowledge of having a personal relationship with Him, I made the best decision of my life. My decision was to learn more about the Bible and to grow closer to God through prayer. Now, I'll share.

I joined an intercessory prayer group at my church. The first night I wanted to go to the prayer meeting, the enemy of my soul threw everything he could at me that night. He caused the disobedience of my children and crazy circumstances to stop me from going that first night. I wasn't able to go because of the "fires" I needed to put out before I would be able to leave the house. The next meeting, I told the enemy of my soul, I was going to the prayer meeting, even if he burned my house down. The circumstances started to mount just as I was preparing to leave, but I spoke out, to the enemy of my soul, that I was going to the prayer meeting anyway. So, I went to the prayer meeting and prayed for the situation I had been dealing with at home. At the meeting that night, I received the Baptism of the Holy Spirit, and was slain in the spirit of God, without the evidence of speaking in tongues. It was an amazing time in the Lord! When I left to go home that evening, everything looked different. It was nighttime but everything seemed brighter than it was when I had arrived earlier that evening. One of the teachings that night was about how powerful the gift of tongues is in the life of a believer. So when I got home that night, I prayed to receive the gift of tongues for my birthday, which happened to be the very next day. I was working and had forgotten all about my prayer to the Lord. I was in my office and I started praying. The gift of tongues fell on me so heavy I couldn't stop speaking in noticeably different languages. Every time I opened my mouth to speak, a different language was coming out. I was even able to sing in these different languages. It was amazing! I left my office with the exciting news, and went to a friend's office, down the hallway, after I thought the experience was over. However, just after I told her I had received the gift of tongues, a foreign language started to come again. She told me to go back to my office and let God finish what He was doing. So, I did what she told me to do. The tongues continued for a short while longer, then ended. I was so excited to let the prayer group know about this amazing experience! I couldn't wait to get to the prayer meeting to share with the group God's birthday present to me.

Trying to get my teenage children settled before leaving the house, for my intercessory prayer meeting, was a major challenge. Our prayer group had started having "Life in the Spirit" (LIS) seminars, and we were forming other LIS prayer groups, at churches around the city. I was always late getting to the prayer meetings or seminars, due to spiritual warfare at home. I started praying to have a parking space in front of the church when I arrived. I knew being late would cause me to have to park a distance from the meetings or seminars. I really didn't want to be walking the unsafe streets alone. God would always provide a parking space, right in front of the church, where the event was being held. It happened every single time. When we would come out from the meeting or seminar, my prayer partners would question, "How did you get that parking space in front of the church when you came so late?" I would tell them, "I prayed, trusted, and I believed God would meet my need, to have a parking spot that was safe, since I was by myself." Up until this very day, whenever I ask for a parking spot close by, especially at night, God provides. Most times, I get the parking spot while others are still looking for one, and If I have to walk a little before reaching my destination, I feel safe, with His hand of protection covering me. God is faithful!

I was on my way home from work one day, and while going through the Metro train gate, I walked up on one of my prayer partners. She had recently lost all of her furniture and personal items in a fire at her home. Now that the renovations were complete, she was ready to get new furniture to replace what had been destroyed. She needed to get furniture delivered to her home on a specific day and at a specific time, due to her schedule. There was no other date or time when it could be delivered. While we were talking, I spoke to God to stop the rain, so that she could get the furniture that she needed. Shortly after the prayer, while we were conversing, the rain stopped. I was facing the outside so I could see what the weather was doing. She had her back to the outside. I told her to turn around and look. She turned and had a shocked look on her face. Jesus told us to ask and we shall receive. I also told her, the Word of God tells us, He will provide for all our needs. Just believe you will receive, and it shall be done.

My daughter had just delivered her first baby. This was my first grandchild! I was a proud Nana, so I took a lot of pictures. This was during the days when pictures were taken with a camera and film from the camera needed to be developed. My sister was out of town at an AZUSA conference and it was her daughter's birthday. We as a family typically get together for birthday celebrations with dinner, cake and ice cream. Since her mother was out of town, I was going to have the birthday celebration at my home. My plan was to go to church, then stop at the grocery store. I would also drop the film off to be developed at a one-hour film developing store, before going home to prepare the food and party table. After church, I was on my way to the Walmart closest to my home but decided to go to the Walmart that I thought was closer to the church. On my way there, I heard a voice that I wasn't sure was the Holy Spirit, tell me to go to the Walmart closest to my house. Leaning to my own understanding, I told myself, that the one I was headed to, was the closest one to the church. The ride became longer than I had imagined, and I heard the voice speak to me again saying, "go to the Walmart closest to your house." I dismissed the thought again and wondered, was God telling me to continue to the one closest to the church or go to the one nearest to my house. As I approached the parking lot of the Walmart closest to the church, I asked God to provide me a parking spot. All spots were taken, except for one. I pulled in feeling extremely blessed since I was able to find a parking spot immediately. As I pulled into the spot, I looked at the license plate of the van in front of where I was parked and it read, "LISTEN." I chuckled when I read it but started to question what God was saying. I started saying to myself, "should I leave and go to the store closest to home, or should I go into the store where I was parked?" I decided to go into the store where I was parked. When I walked into the store, I had to go all the way to the back of the store to discover that the film developing machine was broken. As I walked back to the front door, through the store, on my way back to the car, I was feeling badly. All I could think about was wasting time and not being able to accomplish the things I had set out to do. I heard the still small voice telling me, "if you don't listen to what I tell you with the little things, how are you going to be able to listen, when I tell you more important things?" Immediately, I was convicted that God was trying to save me from the hour I had wasted. I had driven all the way out of my way, to do what I eventually ended up doing at the Walmart nearest, to my house. Also, the grocery store was right across the parking lot from the Walmart store, so I was able to get what I needed, within the hour that it took, to develop the film. After I got home, I fixed the birthday meal and everything else worked in my favor to allow me to have the birthday celebration as planned.

On Time God

God loves a cheerful giver, but when the funds are low and the demands are high, it's sometimes challenging to smile and deliver hard, earned cash to the collection plate. It's a fact that bill collectors don't care about your commitment to tithing or giving offerings. Glad that God is an on-time God! Always working on our behalf, in the times of trouble!

It was the first of the month and the mortgage was due. I needed to mail my mortgage payment, on that particular day, for it to get to its destination on time. It was raining so hard outside in such a short period of time that the weather station on TV was warning that some areas would experience flooding. I was busy doing my chores around the house when I remembered I had to get to the post office to mail my mortgage. My children were young at the time, so I had to gather them together and get through the rain to the car parked in my driveway on the side of the house. We carried our umbrellas and scurried to the car, jumped in, backed out of the driveway and pulled off. The rain was pouring down, and at one point, I could not see the car in front of me. I needed to slow down. All I could think about is my need to get to the post office before they closed their doors. All four of my children were quiet in the back seat of the car. We were experiencing the hard downpours of rain, the wind blowing, and the traffic swishing through the streets as we traveled to our destination. We were one block from the post office, at a four way Stop sign.

Although it was only one block from the post office, the clock was ticking, and the post office would be closing, in just a few minutes. There was a puddle of water in the middle of the intersection, but it didn't look deep, so I drove through it. As soon as I got to the middle of the intersection, my car cut off. Evidently, there was a part of the engine that could not get wet, or else the car would cut off. Unfortunately, I didn't know about it. Here we were stuck in the middle of the intersection with no other cars in sight. All of a sudden, I could feel the car being pushed from behind. As soon as my car was pushed to the other side of the street, clearing the puddle of water, the engine started up again. As we were being pushed, I was praising God for the kindness of a stranger! I turned completely around to see who had pushed us. I just wanted to thank the person for their kindness. But there wasn't anyone around. I didn't see anyone, nor did I hear anyone. There were no cars or people moving about. Then I remembered, I didn't have time to think about what had just happened anymore. I only had a couple of minutes to get to the post office before the doors closed. I started driving the one block necessary to arrive before the closing time. Needless to say, we were blessed by the kindness of an angel. We reached the post office and mailed the mortgage on-time.

One night, I was sleeping and having a strange dream. I dreamt that I was walking through a shoe store with someone I knew, but I didn't see the person's face. As I was walking through, I thought it was strange that all of the shoes looked like boots; tall boots, short boots and pointed boots. It was like walking in a black and white movie. We went to the back of the store where there was a stairway. While walking up the stairway, the dream changed from black and white to color. When we got to the top of the stairs, we were in a place that looked like a library. The library had seating all around the staircase. We sat down to have a conversation about the Lord. While I was talking, I heard laughing noises coming from the downstairs store. The more I talked about Jesus, the more sounds of jeering and laughter I heard. It became so annoying to me that I leaned over the staircase and yelled down the stairs, "STOP!" At that very moment, I heard the jeering and laughing getting closer to me and something attacked me and started to cut off my breathing. I was struggling for air but was unable to get any air because of the attack. I tried to yell out loud but was unable to scream. Then, I started yelling, "JESUS" in my mind and spirit. Immediately, the overwhelming smothering stopped. I woke up able to breathe without any problems. It felt so real! I got up and started praising God as I walked around my house blessing it. JESUS, our Savior, Deliverer, and On-Time God!

When I was five years old, we only had one bathroom in our house, and it was on the second floor. One evening, I went upstairs to use the bathroom. Immediately as I sat on the toilet, the bathroom light went out. I was scared sitting in the dark. I yelled downstairs to my mother to tell her the light was out. She yelled back upstairs, "I'll be there in a minute." Soon, she arrived with the hassock to stand on, and the new lightbulb. As she stood up on the hassock, I heard a voice say, "cover your eyes, the bulb is going to break." Without thinking, I covered my eyes. Suddenly the lightbulb fell to the floor and broke into many pieces. I could feel the pieces pop up after it broke but I did not get cut by the broken pieces. My mother shouted, "don't get up; stay seated until I clean up the glass." So, I stayed seated until my mother had replaced the lightbulb and cleaned up the glass. I never thought again about the voice I heard that night until I attended a School of the Prophets and I was told that God has had His hand on me since I was five years old. I remembered this incident and one other that had happened when I was five. He is truly and on-time God!

One evening during the summer, my children, a couple neighbors, and I were sitting in my sunroom which was in the back of the house. We heard a loud crack of thunder so we turned off the electricity, which was what folks did at that time, while experiencing a thunderstorm. We were having a lively conversation when we heard a huge bolt of lightning crack. It was so loud and close that we were sure it had hit the bottom of my house. I smelled something burning but figured the hard rain would put out any fire. As the rain poured down, a large tree, on the side of my house closest to the sunroom and deck, toppled over towards my next-door neighbor's pool. We heard the tree fall but waited until the storm subsided to go out to see the damage. As I opened the back door, I saw that the bulk of the tree, its branches and its leaves were laying in and across his pool. We could see that the lightning had struck the base of the tree and burned the tree's roots, leaving a large black hole that was still smoldering from the lightning bolt. It could have been the other way. The tree could have toppled over on the sunroom where we were gathered. I started thanking God that the tree did not fall on my home. We were amazed at God's love for us and His protection! He is truly an on-time God!

Miracle Worker

One morning in February, I slipped on black ice, trying to get to my car, on my way to work. My legs left the ground and I fell directly on my left side. As I laid there I was thinking, "does anything hurt?" I tried moving my limbs and I didn't feel any pain, so I got up off of the ground. However, when I stood up, my left arm was throbbing with pain. Although I heard the still small voice tell me to, "go back in the house and call the doctor", I got into my car anyway, because I wanted to go to my office downtown to work. I didn't feel that the pain I was feeling, at that moment, necessitated going inside and calling the doctor. At that very moment, I was making the mistake of leaning to my own understanding instead of listening to the still small voice whose purpose is to lead, guide and direct us to all truth. (Proverbs 3:5-6) I was actually trying to get some space from my mother. I had brought her to my house to stay with me, to make sure she was safe, during the terrible snowstorm that left the residents in our area barricaded in our homes, for several days. Government offices were closed for four days. Many businesses closed their doors, for at least three days. Everyone was trying to dig out of the close to three feet of snow that had fallen during the storm.

On the way to my office, I kept telling myself I was going to be fine, since I didn't feel the pain of having broken bones. I arrived at my office and settled in. I had the peace and serenity I desired but by the end of the workday, I was in quite a bit of pain. I was glad it was Friday. I just wanted to get home and start my weekend, hoping the pain would clear up, after medication and rest.

After I went back to work, the pain returned and intensified. I was in a lot of pain while sitting at my office desk typing on the computer. The pain I was experiencing necessitated a call to my doctor for an appointment. After going to the doctor, the following week, he told me I needed to have an MRI. The scan showed I had injured two disks in my neck. The two disks affected my left and right shoulders, arms and hands. I was given the option of having surgery to correct the issue. After discussing the options with my doctor, I was advised not to have surgery unless I could not move my arms and legs, because surgery could make my situation either better or worse. I opted not to have the surgery, because it would only temporarily correct the problem. I decided to trust God to heal me through natural methods.

God knew this accident was going to happen and He had already worked this situation for His glory. I was blessed to find out that my job had just signed a contract for employees to get six months of short-term disability insurance shortly before this accident. So, I was blessed to be on short term sick leave from my job for six months, as I healed. While I was recuperating at home, I was getting all kinds of natural medical treatments. All of these extra treatments cost much more than I could afford. I didn't know what I was going to do. But I did know, God had a plan. Receiving a paycheck every two weeks through the short-term medical insurance my agency provided, helped me pay for the medical expenses.

It was also a blessing that one of my daughters freed her schedule to drive me to my acupuncture appointment once a week for two months. It took two-hours to drive, round trip, not including the thirty-minute treatment time. Fortunately, after two months of acupuncture treatments, I didn't feel any pain, except when turning my neck from side to side. While visiting my massage therapist, she recommended an incredible chiropractor to help with my healing. I went to the chiropractor weekly. I was excited that after only two weeks of adjustments, I got the mobility back in my neck. Unfortunately, I incurred muscular atrophy from laying down for two months, after only getting up to eat and use the bathroom. This physical ailment caused an inability to do several things including simple household tasks. However, God sent one of my neighbors to help me with grocery shopping. She was truly a Godsend!

Other practical things were left undone. One of those things was getting my hair washed. Due to the injury, I couldn't lift my arms high enough and for long enough to do it myself. I had been going to the hair salon to have my hair fixed prior to the accident. Once I got the mobility back in my neck, I needed my hair washed. One day as I was leaving my primary care doctor's office. I was praying to ask God about getting my hair washed.

On my way home, as I was driving down a residential street, when it started to drizzle. The wind was blowing very gently. I didn't see anyone walking on the sidewalk, in the doorway, or in any of the windows of the homes, in the neighborhood where I was driving. As I was driving down the street, the gentle wind blew two pieces, of what looked like money, straight down in the street directly in front of me. The drizzle held the two pieces to the street. My curiosity made me pull over to the curve and park so I could get out of the car to investigate what had just dropped from the sky. As I approached it, I could see that it was two twenty-dollar bills. No one was walking or driving at this time. It was just me, some trees, and the sky above. I picked up the money and asked the Lord what He wanted me to do with it. He answered, "Go get your hair done." Getting my hair fixed, at that time, costs me exactly forty dollars. I got into my car and drove off to the hair salon praising God for His faithfulness. Needless to say, God was with me during the entire seven years it took for my neck to completely heal. He took care of every detail of every need in my life at that time. God is simply awesome!

When I was five years old, we lived in the middle house of three row houses with one of my mother's brothers and his family on one side and another one of my mother's brothers and his family was on the other side. Both brother's wives, who were my Aunts, were our babysitters at one time or another. This particular day, I was next door at my aunt on the left side of our house because she was the babysitter that day. It was in the morning before school and my aunt was preparing breakfast in the kitchen. One of the little girls who was there under my aunt's care, and myself, began to play a game of hide and seek. I got the bright idea to hide under the kitchen table. There was a tablecloth on the table, so I was being hidden by it. After a while, I had been waiting a long time and the little girl didn't come to find me. I decided to leave the space under the table and go back into the living room. As I came out from under the table, my aunt had just taken a hot pot of oatmeal off of the stove and was walking towards the table to fill the bowls for our breakfast. When I stood up, my head hit the scalding hot pot and my aunt couldn't hold on to the pot, so it turned over on my head. I was screaming to the top of my lungs. My aunt immediately dropped the pot, picked me up and put my head under the faucet of cold running water. While my aunt was holding me under the cold water, I was hollering and screaming. She urgently yelled out to my uncle to call my mother before she left for work. My mother came running over from next door and took me across the street to the doctor's office. After examining the burns, the doctor proclaimed, "young lady you are very lucky. If your aunt hadn't acted so quickly by putting your head under the cold faucet to get the oatmeal off of your skin, you would have sustained third degree burns all over your head and forehead. Instead, you have first and second-degree burns. Your hair and forehead will have scabs but will not be affected by this burn. No hair loss and no permanent scars." Today, there are no signs of that oatmeal accident. God had His hand on me! God is an awesome God! He is indeed a miracle worker!

Promise Keeper

God is not a man that He should lie. Sometimes you may be following something you think is God but find out, as you follow that path, that it wasn't God after all. Then, you feel as if you have been running around on a gerbil's wheel or chasing a mirage. You're in a cycle. God's way is not our way. His ways and thoughts are higher than ours. He tells us we must not lean on our own understanding rather trust Him and He will work it out for our good and His glory.

God promises He will never leave us nor forsake us. He will always be with us, until the end of time. What a mighty God we serve! He's our Father, Abba. Always on-time, compassionate, loving, caring, nurturing, protecting, healing, covering and I could go on and on about how awesomely, wonderful our God is to us! Most of all, every promise He makes, He keeps!

After more projects than I could keep up with, my money-pit house went into foreclosure. My children and I had to move out. I didn't want to move out of Maryland. There were too many changes that had to be made, including changing schools, vehicle tags, and car pools. My sister was living in a Section 8 townhome housing development in Virginia. She encouraged me to put my name on the list at the development four years prior because I was no longer receiving child support payments and was struggling to pay the mortgage and keep up with the home repair projects. The Virginia townhome housing development staff called me every year to see if I was still interested in staying on the list. One year, I told them to take my name off the list because I had earned a promotion and didn't think I qualified for the program anymore. However, there came a time, shortly thereafter, when I could no longer make the mortgage payments on my home, due to the home repair projects. I decided it best to move into a more affordable home so I started looking for another place to live. I put the house up for sale. I was hopeful that someone would buy it. I had assumed a Veteran's loan on the home and unfortunately, the previous owner had passed away a couple of years prior. The previous owner and his wife did not disclose that the house was a money pit. It had been placed up for sale a second time and they just wanted to get rid of it.

The owner was dying and needed to move to Arizona to extend his life. My heart went out to them about this situation and was a determining factor in my decision to purchase the home. I felt like we were helping each other. Unfortunately, the previous owner only lived a few more years after moving to Arizona.

I prayed and prayed for God to give me a house in the same county where I was living so that I wouldn't have to make all of those state required changes. I called realtors from all over the area, but none responded. I started to panic because the end of the month was near and I needed to move. If I didn't sell the house, foreclosure was imminent. I called the Section 8 townhome development to see if I had a status on the list for move-ins. Although I had asked the office to take my name off of the list the year before; but GOD....I was still on the list. The miracle was that I was next on the list! A house that had been vacant for almost six months due to major destruction from a previous tenant had just been renovated and it was available. I should have been jumping for joy, but I was not. I did not want to move out of Maryland. The door was open in Virginia, yet I still called more real estate agents to see if someone could find me a house in my desired area. Again, no one responded. I had to accept the fact that the house in Virginia was my open door.

I hadn't saved enough money to pay the security deposit and first month's rent. I was financially embarrassed with no conceivable way out yet I didn't want to make all of the adjustments necessary when moving to another state. I was as foolish as foolish could be at that time. I didn't see the blessings waiting for me and my family in Virginia. The Townhome Section 8 housing development called me on a Wednesday and told me I could come to sign the papers for the house on Friday. Friday morning, before the appointment, I went to one of my work friends who was also one of my car poolers and told her the dilemma. Her advice was for me to go through the open door and see what God had for me. I took her advice and walked through the open door. The housing development manager made arrangements for me to pay the total amount in installments so that I could move in on that same day. The Section 8 stipend provided $50 per month to help pay the rent. The rent for the townhome included the gas and water bills. I only had to pay the electric bill. With just a little help, I was able to get back on my feet. God had worked it out!

Not only did I get blessed, but my obedience caused a blessing for one of my carpoolers. She was a single parent with two children. She needed a futon so that her children could watch television and play in the basement of her home. She only had $100 to spend on it. While I was signing my paperwork for my townhome rental, a woman getting ready to move out of the complex came into the office asking if anyone needed a brand new futon for $100. I let her know I was interested in seeing it for my carpooler to purchase. Needless to say, the same day I was moving into my townhome, she was picking up the futon. Not only did she get the futon but the lady had several brand new small appliances she decided to give away. The lady was relocating and moving in with her father so she didn't need them. My car pooler told me all of the new appliances were the ones she needed to replace in her kitchen.

Another big blessing was that I used to be the taxi running all of my children back and forth to their after schools activities and their jobs. After moving, I found out that Virginia schools had after school buses so they were able to ride the bus before and after school. Also, each of them found a job the first time they went out looking on a Sunday. The jobs, during the summer, were in walking distance to our community so they were able to walk. Hallelujah! God knew I needed all of these things to give me an opportunity to rest. He has our best interest at heart. He undoubtedly has kept all of His promises to me with my house situation, at that time, and in everything else that concerns my life. He is truly a promise keeper!

Light In The Darkness

God shines His light in the darkness to illuminate truth. Anything done in darkness will come to the light. In the past, I used to believe I needed to keep my personal life quiet. Nobody needed to know who I was dating or whether I was dating at all. It wasn't the person's business, it was mine. As I grew closer to the Lord, I discovered that God already knows all, and sees all. There is nothing hidden from Him. No secret places. Everything is an open book to Him. He doesn't look at or focus on the outward appearance of a person, like man does. God reads our hearts. He sees every nook and cranny. Nothing goes unnoticed. If we ask Him, He will show us a person's heart. Just wait quietly while a person is talking. Listen carefully to what the person is saying. They may not realize what they are saying at the time, but they are speaking their heart about a person, or situation. Matthew 12:34b states, "for out of the abundance of the heart, the mouth speaks." (NKJV) It's also interesting to note, that our eyes are the windows to our souls. When we look into someone's eyes, we can gather their well-being. We can see truth and error. Darkness and light can be seen in our eyes.

I bought a Toyota C-HR SUV Crossover for my birthday! It was a little more compact, and sporty than the previous SUV I had purchased and the closest thing to a sports car I could afford. My father used to drive race cars in his early adulthood, so I guess I got that desire gene from him. I absolutely loved looking at it and driving it! I picked it out of a book at the dealership and knew right away it was the one for me! I had been driving a SUV since my children started going to college over fifteen years ago, but had decided to down-size a bit since I no longer needed the extra space provided by the traditional SUV. I knew right away, at this season of my life, the C-HR Crossover was the perfect one for me. The C-HR was eight weeks old before I took it to the car wash for its first bath. The day after the car wash, I came outside to see bird poop down the front of the car and the window on the driver's side of the car. When I saw this, my first reaction was surprise, but I quickly remembered, when I was a teenager, where the birds had their wicked way with something else I owned, so I just chuckled.

I had bought a white polyester, hot pants jumpsuit with a super-sized large, red heart on the front centered in the middle of the top portion. I loved that outfit! When I would wash it and hang it out on the clothesline in the back yard to dry, each time, it seemed as if the birds would aim for the heart and poop on it. After a few times of this happening, I wised up and decided that after I washed it, I would hang it up in the basement to dry. The problem was solved. Applying that same strategy for my car, I needed to either move my car to another parking space and hope the birds wouldn't recognize it or buy a house with a garage. I chose to get a house with a garage since the car would be protected from all of the outside elements as well as the birds, who seemed to love it as much as I do. I haven't gotten that home with the garage yet, so I still experience the bird's way of showing me love, but one day I will have a garage and out smart the birds.

Nuggets Of Encouragement For The Journey

After you make the bold, courageous decision to become a Christian by fully accepting Jesus into your heart as Lord and Savior, and being baptized by water and the fire of the Holy Spirit, you have already won the victory over every problem, situation or circumstance in your past, present and future! You become one with Jesus and are now one of God's children inheriting the promises God has for all of His children. It may have been the hardest decision of your life but the benefits are eternal!

Walking away from a lifestyle that is not pleasing to God can be tough, but you will come to understand that it is the best decision you have made in your life! Jesus has already won every battle you will ever have to fight! He loves us with an everlasting, unconditional love. No matter what we have said or done or the things in the future we might do, He will always love us. God is love!

The Bible admonishes Christians, in this life, first to love God and worship and praise Him above all people and things. Next, to love our neighbors as ourselves. Our neighbors are everyone else on earth. Christians must also grow in the truth and the faith of God's Word by reading, hearing and practicing the teachings in the Bible, God's Word. The Bible also admonishes us to be baptized in the Holy Spirit to operate in the power of the fruit of God's Spirit; love, joy, peace, patience, kindness, goodness, faithfulness, gentleness and self-control. Galatians 5:22-23. God gives these gifts to strengthen us for our journey through the challenges of life.

After we have been baptized by water and by the fire of the Holy Spirit, we go through the process of growth as a new babe in Christ. First, we "sip on the spiritual milk," which is learning and growing in our faith in the Word of God. Eventually, we grow and mature in our understanding and application of the Word of God. Then, we will feast on the "meat" of God's Word, His anointed, powerful teachings. They will help us to live in peace as we war against the enemy and to live the abundant, victorious life God desires for each one of us. God is passionate about us obtaining wisdom and knowledge about the necessary tools He has given us to win every battle. God gave us Jesus in our hearts, the indwelling of the Holy Spirit in our spirit, and a personal relationship with Him as our Father which allows us access to God 24/7.

Moreover, God has promised His children a rich inheritance, strategically thought out and executed without flaw, by sacrificing His only Son Jesus the Christ. Through Jesus' death and resurrection, all of God's children are promised eternal life. God had a plan for us before He formed us in our mother's womb. It's our job to walk out our individualized destiny, in reverential fear and trembling before God. We must remember that everything we do is done in the eyesight of God to please Him, not man. Everything we do for God, we do to the best of our ability in excellence. It is our heart's desire to please God. Our expectation and promise at the end of our journey through life, is for our Spirit to transition from our body to be present with the Lord. The Bible tells us to be absent from the body is to be present with the Lord, who is at the right hand of the Father, in all of His glory. He is the King of Kings and Lord of Lords! It is by faith that we anticipate during our transition into eternity, hearing God say, "Welcome, my good and faithful servant, enter In."

Problems

When you realize God is bigger than anything, you can put God over all things and realize there is nothing impossible with God, and absolutely nothing bigger than God.

Compartmentalize problems to work on each piece, so it won't seem so overwhelming, and it will be solved once all of the pieces are worked out.

Helpmeet

God is love! He created man in His own image and out of love for man, God put the man to sleep and took man's rib to create a woman. She is to be known as his helpmeet. She was taken from man, who was created in God's image. She is also created in God's own image. The woman was taken from the man's rib to walk beside him and together with love, in love, by love, have dominion over all things. Both were created for God's purpose. Equally essential in the eyesight of God (1 Corinthians 13: 4-8a). Men who hear from God and truly want a wife, know when they have found their rib. Wait on the Lord and be of good courage. Wait, I say, on the Lord.

Finding your forever love is a byproduct of finding your first true love, the creator and lover of our souls. Everyone and everything else, is secondary. When we seek and find the true lover of our souls, that connection draws the desired earthly love connections to us.

Adam left Eve unattended long enough for the snake to convince her that what God had told Adam about the tree of life was not true. The enemy was able to change her mindset from what Adam, her husband, had told her. Adam must have been a workaholic tending to the things of the garden and animals more than the needs of his wife, making it easy for the snake to smooth talk her into sin. What God told Adam and Eve was the key to an abundant and fruitful life. If Adam had been the head and priest of his home, he would have manifested the goodness of God in their lives to Eve. Adam was charged with lifting up God's Words in repetition to keep a balance in their home. He was responsible for communicating with his wife daily, making sure the enemy could not get a foothold into his relationship with his wife, and gain a place in his marriage.

Timing

In My timing, not yours, you will see My glory. From the rising of the sun till the going down of the same, My Word is everlasting. It's a still small voice, not a raging wave. From glory to glory My name is to be praised. Think not on the things of the past, for I'm doing a new thing in your life. Prepare for the battle. Put on your armor. My thoughts are not your thoughts. My ways are not your ways; they are higher. How can you move a mountain if you have not the faith of a mustard seed? Increase your faith. Grow nigh unto Me. I will show you all you need to know when the time is right. My time is not your time. Keep growing in knowledge and the understanding of Me. I will help you to see My glory. Be steadfast, unmovable. Don't let anyone steal your joy. You are precious in My sight. Keep up the good work. I Am proud of you. Stay connected to the vine. I will shower you with My love for now and evermore. I will strengthen you for your journey. I will help you. Be confident in who you are and whose you are. You will continue to learn and grow for such a time as this. I will not tarry. I will move swiftly. You will do My will, as I have purposed you to. Do not be afraid. I will be with you always. Stay connected. I will never fail you. Enjoy life, friendship. There is much work to do. All will happen in My time. I Am God, above Me there is no other. I Am that I Am. Trust Me with all of your heart and lean not to your own understanding, in all your ways acknowledge Me and I shall direct your path. I Am the cornerstone, the rock that the builders rejected. Above Me there is no other. Stay in My presence. I will reveal what you need to know, in My presence.

Worry

Do not fear; I Am with you. I Am the Alpha and the Omega; The first and the last. I can do all things so, why should you worry or fret? Listen to My instruction: Seek ye first the kingdom of heaven and all else will follow. I Am not a man that I should tell a lie. Growth is important, My love. I will not forsake you. (1 John 3:2-3)

Listen

Eyes have not seen, nor ears heard, the wonderful things that I have planned for you! If you will listen, I will tell you. Don't share everything I tell you with others. This is between you and Me. Wait on the Lord and be of good courage. Just wait on Me. The devil is a liar! There is no truth in him. Don't go by the way a situation looks. Things aren't always as they seem. Be anxious for nothing, but for all things give honor, glory and praise. Trust Me. I will not let them snatch you out of My hand.

Everlasting Love

Be ye ever ready. Beloved, I stand at the door and knock. Will you let Me in? In a moment, in a twinkling of an eye, I will be with you. I Am the Alpha and Omega, the first and the last. You can do all things through Me. Do not be afraid. I Am with you always. Nothing is too hard for Me! I love you with and everlasting love. I love, honor, and respect you. As a husband loves his wife, so I love you. And even more for I will never leave you, nor forsake you as long as you live. Abide in Me as I abide in you. You will have everlasting peace. I Am the vine, you are the branches, stay connected to the vine for everlasting life. Fire. Holy Ghost fire. I will never leave you nor forsake you. Stay close.

Focus

Focus on Me and My will. I will never leave you nor forsake you. I Am your bridge over troubled waters. I am the way, the truth, and the light. No one comes to the Father except through Me. Your body is a temple of the Holy Spirit. Do not grieve the Holy Spirit by which you were sealed for the day of redemption. Be not afraid. I go before you always. Come follow Me and I will give you rest. Contentment of heart, will I give you.

I Am the Alpha and the Omega, the first and the last. Jesus is the light of the world. There is no darkness in Him. I love you with an everlasting love. Eyes have not seen, nor ears heard the things I have prepared for you. Keep your light shining bright. No matter what happens, keep your light shining bright. I will never leave you, nor forsake you. For I Am that light of the world!

I Am higher than the heavens and the earth! There is none greater than Me! Don't be afraid for I Am with you always. From the rising of the sun until the going down of the same. I Am worthy of your praise. Do not forsake the assembly of the saints. You will know them by their love, unconditional love. I will love you with an everlasting love. Be steadfast, unmovable. (Ephesians 6:10-18)

New Beginning

I Am the Alpha and the Omega. Nothing comes before Me. A new beginning. The old has passed away, behold all things are new.

I love you with an everlasting love. You are the apple of My eye. Come to Me all who are heavily burdened, and I will give you rest. Trust Me with all your heart, I will never leave you nor forsake you. I Am the Alpha and the Omega, the first and the last. Old things have passed away, behold all things are new. Stay connected. Peace be with you, My child. I love you. Don't forget it. Keep Me close to your heart. I will never fail you. Your growth is important. I will work it out, concerning your children. You can do all things through Christ who strengthens you. Be not dismayed or upset. If I give it to you to do, I will equip you for every good work.

For I know the plans I have for you, plans for good and not evil. Listen, take heed. All the earth is mine. I bring all things into being. All life, all holiness is from me. Take My yoke upon you for My yoke is easy and My burden is light. Rest beside the still waters to refresh your soul. Nothing is lacking in those who are in Me; who wait upon Me. Do not concern yourself with the things of this present world. Grow in the love and admonition of My son Jesus. Nothing is lacking for those who are in Him. The Holy Spirit is your comforter. He refreshes your soul! Hallelujah to the new, born King! Pray without ceasing for your adversary, the devil, lurks around you. Be still and know that I Am God! I work all things for your good and My Glory. Connect the dots. From glory to glory. Each step shows forth new meaning. One step at a time. Be anxious for nothing. Your Father is quite capable of taking care of you. He loves you dearly. You are His daughter, and He loves you. Rest assured what you know in your heart is of Me.

For we walk by faith and not by sight. I purposed you and fashioned you, when I knit you in your Mother's womb. We all desire someone to love us with a love so deep and sure. You find that love in Me. Man's love is fickle. He can't promise you the love that only I can give. I will supply all of your needs just as I promised long ago. Peace be with you always. Never worry. Never doubt. I will always bring you out.

Be Still

Be still and know that I Am God. I love you with an everlasting love. Have faith in Me. I clothe the lilies of the valley and I lead all souls to the Father.

Be still and know that I Am God. I Am Lord of the wind and rain. I can do it!

Be still and know that I Am God. Worship and adore Me. Praise Me in the sanctuary. Lessons learned are precious in My sight. I know every bump and bruise. I know your frustrations when you lay down and get up. Leave them all with Me, the guardian of your soul. Fear not, because I Am with you always, until the end of time. You are Mine and I love you with an everlasting love. Be steadfast and unmovable, always abiding in My love for you. Be of good cheer because I have conquered everything that troubles you. I Am God and nothing is too hard for Me. Everything is possible with Me. I will lead and guide you to all truth. Trust Me.

I Am the Lord your God; there are none like Me. Relax and know that I Am God. I created the heavens with My right hand. Is anything too hard for Me? Listen carefully for My voice. I will lead, guide and direct you to all truth. Anything not truth, is not Me. You are the head, and not the tail; the lender, and not the borrower. All power is in My hand. Trust Me. I love you with an everlasting love. Be still and know that I Am Almighty God.

You are My precious jewel. All things work together for the good of those who love Me and are called according to My purposes. Be still and know that I Am God. I work all things for your good, and My glory. This situation is a temporary setback, in preparation for the setup I have for you. Be patient, and learn from Me. I have not forsaken you. Trust Me, and you will see My hand at work. It is well.

For you were bought with a price. Be still and know that I Am God. Do not be afraid. What can man do to you when I Am your God?

On Time

If today you hear His voice, harden not your heart! All things are possible to the one that believes. Hold on to God's never changing hand. He will lead you to all truth. Trust Him. You will not falter. Greater is He who is within you than he who is in this world. My love does not change. I love you with an everlasting love. Be still and know that I Am God. I will do it. You do not have to spend countless hours worrying and wondering about My plans for you. I Am ordering your steps day by day. Keep your mind focused on Jesus and He will do it. Trust and obey. You will not be late. I Am an on-time God. I never miss an appointment. Your destiny is My business. Let Me work it out. I Am the only one who can change hearts and minds. I will fill them with My love, and they will be filled up to overflowing! I delight in blessing My children. When I bring it to you, it will always be good. I only give good gifts to bless and not curse My children. Don't worry. Don't fret. Rest and be at peace; soon. I love when you praise Me. It is music to My ears. I delight in blessing you!

Wait

You are strong in the Lord and the power of His might. All that befalls you will be put to shame. Walk in the light of Christ and you will not fulfill the desires of the flesh. I will hold you up with My mighty right hand. I can work all things out for your good and My Glory. Don't take your eyes off of the prize. Greater is He who is in you than he that is in this present world, which is passing away. Good things shall follow you all of the days of your life for your obedience to My commands. Work it out. Problems will come, but I Am able to deliver you from them all. Be anxious for nothing. Be patient and wait on the Lord. He will love you with an everlasting love. You will be blessed coming in and blessed going out. Your enemies will be your footstools. He who hates Me hates the world I created, as well as My people. He comes to put you in bondage. I came to set you free! Be strong in the Lord and in the power of His might. All is well! Wait on Me.

They that wait on the Lord shall renew their strength. They shall mount up on wings like an eagle and soar. They shall run and not be weary. They shall walk and never faint. Wait on the Lord just a little while longer. Trust and believe, My friend. He will work it out for you. Hold on a little while longer.

Trust

I Am Master, Ruler, and Savior over all men. Hearken to My voice when I speak, and you will be following the truth. Many have spoken who are false prophets and they seek to lead you astray. I Am the Good Shepherd and I will only lead you to the truth that My father has told Me. Glory to God in the highest for the things He has done! He is moving mountains on your behalf to see to it that you will arrive at your destination on time. He has not forgotten you or the things you have been through to further the kingdom. He delights in you and enjoys your presence. The time you spend with Him. Listen to Him when He speaks to you and you will never go wrong. Eyes have not seen, and ears have not heard, the things He has planned for your life. Be persistent in well doing. You shall reap when the time of harvest arrives. Walk in the love of the Lord always, no matter the situation, call on Me to strengthen you to walk in love – for love is of Me and I commanded you to walk in love from the beginning. All of My children should walk in love, especially towards those who don't know love. I love you with an everlasting love! Be ye ever ready for you know not the day or the hour of

My visitation. Pack your bags and be ready to go wherever I send you. You are a messenger of truth. Wherever you go, know that I Am with you always. Fear not the days of small beginnings.

I love you with an everlasting love! No one can change how I feel about you, My precious one. Like days of old, you can trust Me to be there whenever you need Me. I will shower you with the grace and mercy you need whenever you need it. Just ask and I will supply your every need. Your heart is so big, and you are able to love many people. You forgive easily too. You will bless My people going in and coming out. I will supply all that you need to be successful in all of your endeavors. You have a heart that reaches out and blesses others with faithfulness in abundance. Your intense love will be rewarded. Wait on Me to bring all things to fulfillment. You love Me with an everlasting love. Continue to pray and worship Me in the beauty of holiness. Be anxious for nothing. In due season, I will supply. Bask in My presence to fulfill your heart's deepest desires. A longing for Me; a thirst for Me. Your soul will never run dry, for I will continuously bring forth rivers of water flowing to and from it. Stay in My presence and serve Me always. Don't move to the left or the right. My love is constant, so must your love be constant.

I love you with an everlasting love. If you can just receive that message deep within your heart and being, you will trust Me more. I'm not trying to hurt you, rather give you life, more abundantly. Focus on Me and what I Am doing in your life, and you will not fear. I stand in proxy for everyone who has hurt you to say, "I am sorry." May My healing touch penetrate and permeate through your heart, mind, soul, spirit, and your entire being. Feel the Balm of Gilead healing your past hurts and sufferings. Today is the day to rejoice! Rejoice in Jesus your Savior! Rejoice that you have been given Salvation through My Son! Rejoice that your name has been written in the Lambs Book of Life! Rejoice that your family's names will be written there as well! May My Father's perfect will be done in your life today and always. He has His hands on you. He said He will see you through. Count on His direction to lead you where you need to go to do whatever I want you to do in My name. Suffer the little children to come to Me.

I love them and will keep them in My hands, leading them as they grow.

Do not fret over the small things. I Am all powerful and able to work out any problem or situation. Just trust Me. I never waiver. Love Me with all of your heart, mind and strength, and I will delight you with blessings beyond measure. Take courage. I have overcome the world!

Be not weary in well doing, for you shall reap a harvest in due season. Grow in the love and admonition of the Lord. Be not afraid or distraught. You shall reap if you faint not. I Am the Alpha and the Omega, first and last. Be not troubled by what you see with your eyes. Open your heart to the love I have for you, and trust and believe all that I have told you, for it will come to past. I Am, that I Am. You are fearfully and wonderfully made. Rest in Me, your fortress and your deliverer. Trust Me in all things. I will never leave you, nor forsake you. You can count on Me, to always be there for you.

I Am the Lord thy God. I love you with an everlasting love. I Am the Alpha and the Omega; first and last. Trust Me and do not be afraid. What can man do to you? I Am with you always. All things work together for the good of those who love Me and are called according to My purpose. Be patient. I'm working things out for your good and My glory! You shall fly! Running from Me only delays the process. Be strong in the Lord and the power of His might. I will see you through it all. Trust Me. Without a doubt, I will bring you out to safety and assurance. You are My workmanship. I'm creating in you a clean heart and renewing your mind. Love is in the air! Walk in it. You will not falter or faint. I will hold you up with My righteous right hand. Sorrow is a part of life, but you will have joy again; abundantly. Hold on to My never changing hand. I will take you on a journey like never before. Peace be with you and Shalom is the banner.

Direction

My child, eyes have not seen, nor ears heard the blessings I have in store for you! Like a child unwrapping gifts on Christmas Day, you will unwrap your gifts and use them to the Glory of God! Be not afraid of wrongdoing. You are covered in My blood and your fleece is as white as snow. Struggle no longer with the things from your past. This is an everlasting love and I will show you a manifestation of My love in days to come. Be not afraid of doing well. Success is of Me and you wear it well! Come to Me with a humble and contrite spirit and I will give you rest. Worship Me only, in Spirit and in truth. I Am leading you down a path of righteousness. Follow My lead and you will never falter. I Am the one leading, guiding and directing you. Rest easy and be assured I love you and will catch you before you fall. Keep your eyes on Me and you will not get confused about all of the other persons who would like to direct your life. I Am the only one who has the true plan for your life. Listen to Me, and I will direct your paths on the narrow road.

Do not be afraid. I Am with you always. I Am leading you to a place of green pastures and a land flowing with milk and honey. Trust Me. I will never leave you or forsake you. When I say it, it's already done. I have your best interest at heart. It is in My best interest that you do not fail. I need you for such a time as this. Your success is My success. My gain. Humble yourself before man and I will exalt you in due season. Realize life and death is in the power of the tongue and make your words few to those who persecute you. I will exalt you in due season.

I Am that I Am. I know the plans I have for you. Plans for good and not evil. Plans for a successful end. Glorify Me with praise and thanksgiving. With a grateful heart you bless Me. Stand firm in your anointing. Like the Rock of Gibraltar, be not moved. Use My words to create an atmosphere of worship and praise. Allow Me to permeate your Spirit with the fullness of Me. Grow in your discernment of people. Some are good and others are evil. Know the difference. Don't let a smooth-talking person convince you that they are My child. You will know them by their fruit. The fruit of love is evident in all who have My seed in them. All of My children know how to love. Do not be deceived. Walk in the light of My presence and serve Me.

In this time of preparation, you must believe in My promises to get to the next level of understanding. Believing in My Word expands your knowledge and understanding of Me and how I work with you, in you, and through you. Be alert to the tricks of the enemy. It's during these times of testing where believing in My promises will help to develop fruit in you and strength of which joy abounds. Be steadfast and unmovable, always abiding in love. Love is My signature on a life committed to and flowing through the gifts of the spirit growing in you. Be not discouraged or dismayed. I Am still in control. Just as the storm rose up and the winds were blowing out of control and I spoke to them saying, "Peace Be Still." I speak to the storms and winds roaring in your life, through you, using your creative force, your mouth, to command them to "Be Still!" You are My child. No good thing will I withhold from you and no demon from hell will overtake you. Stand firm. Be on guard. I've given you the weapons of warfare to fight every battle. It's not yours to fight. You already have the victory in Christ Jesus. Be still and know that I Am God! All things work together for good for those who are called according to My purpose. Those I call, I equip for every good and perfect work that I will perform through My yielded vessels. Glorify the name of the Lord Jesus! Sing praises to Him and honor Him. He is My Son of which I Am well pleased. He was obedient unto death on the cross. He knew His assignment and He carried it out flawlessly. I give you assignments as well. Listen, be attentive and be obedient to whatever you hear Me say. You are My mouthpiece; My hands, My feet, and you have My heart. Love unconditionally, as I love you. Forgive quickly, and easily to prevent roots of bitterness, resentfulness, anger, jealousy, envy and strife from rooting deeply in your heart, preventing you from gaining all of what I have prepared for you and thwarting the good plan I desire to be accomplished in your life and the other lives you touch. For I know the plans I have for you; plans for good and not evil; plans for an expected end. Walk in the light of My presence and you will not fulfill the lusts of the flesh. It will be far from you. Trust Me in all things. I will never lead you astray. I will be with you through it all. Grow in the admonition of Christ.

When I Am for you, who can be against you? I Am the Bread of Life, eat and be filled! For I know the plans I have for you. Plans for your good and hope for the future. Do not allow the enemy to taint the truth I have placed in you. I Am a jealous God, and I will not allow any idols before Me. Put your life in order with Me first. I Am the Hope of Glory! I Am the answer to all of your problems and questions. I hold the key to every dream or desire you have. I pick up where you end. When you come to the end of yourself, I will be there, in all My Glory, with arms outstretched, waiting for you. I desire to wrap My arms around you and fill you with the peace that passes understanding, and the love that loves past feelings, and pain. A love that never ends.

Press

I Am the Lord your God. Hearken to my voice in the midst of trials and temptations. I will lead you on the steady, narrow path to righteousness, peace and joy. Do not be afraid of the tumultuous days or the nights. I Am with you always. Challenge your faith to rise above the (lackadaisical) and strengthen it by following My every thought that I give you to bless others. My people are in various stages of faith. Use your muscles of faith to press past the simple mountains before you. You are more than a conqueror in Christ Jesus who steadies you in the walk with Me. Greater is He that is in you then He who is in this world. Do not be deceived. God is not mocked. He knows all about your fiery trials and the challenges you are going through. He loves you with an everlasting love and will never forsake you. (Psalm 54, Obadiah & Titus)

Testing

I Am the Lord your God, listen to Me. You have been through many trials and tests and passed with flying colors! Do not slumber during this time of testing. I need you to be alert and ready to move when I speak. It is important for your growth that you not tell everything that I share with you or that I allow to happen during this season. You can be tripped up by those who desire to sift you like wheat; those who don't want you to succeed. You have many gifts and talents that lay dormant. I want to bring you exposure to allow those gifts to manifest. Do not be afraid to follow My voice and whatever I tell you to do. It will be for your good and My glory. Do not despise the day of small beginnings. All things work together for good for those who love Me and are called according to My purpose. As long as you get the message, I Am conveying to you, do not worry about the way I choose to relay it to you. You are blessed of the Lord and highly favored! I love you with an everlasting love. Hearken to My voice for direction. I Am your El Shadi. Pay attention to My voice so you will not follow another. Thank you for getting up early to meet Me in prayer and to glean a word of encouragement to help you make it through this day. I will speak to you concerning the issues of your heart at the appropriate time. Keep the faith and know that I Am with you always. I do not sleep or slumber. I Am fully aware of all of your situations and issues and will address them in due season. Keep alert, until then, which won't be long, I will give you the desires of your heart, in My time, not yours. Be alert, be vigilant, for you know not the day of My visitation. Be ready to take action when I say "move." I will give you the steps to take when the time is right. Rest in My presence and enjoy the blessings I have in store for you. I will manifest myself mightily in you and through you for My glory and honor. (Psalm 139)

Fashioned

I Am the Lord your God, and I love you with an everlasting love. I hurt when you hurt. I laugh when you laugh. I smile when you smile. You are My handiwork. I fashioned you after Myself. You are My ears, eyes, hands, feet and heart. You are special. You are the apple of My eye. Don't allow anyone to tell you differently. What does their opinion mean anyway? I'm the only one you need to please. I Am a jealous God. Have no idols before Me. You are blessed of the Lord and highly favored. Do not doubt. I will bring you out, with bells on! You will shine forth like the rays of day. There is nothing, I cannot do. Do not trust in man. Seek Me with all of your heart. I will never let you down or disappoint you. Stay connected to Me, the vine. You will flourish and grow with the nourishment of My Word. Draw nigh to Me, and I will teach you, and share with you, secrets of an abundant life in Me. My Word spells out everything you need to know. My thoughts, and My ways, are higher than yours, and your interpretation may need some help. Remain status quo.

Visions

My people perish for the lack of knowledge. Those who have the skills are not working them to My Glory. When will they take Me seriously and begin to run with their visions and dreams? I weep over the lack of teachers in a world so needy. When will they pick up the torch and run with it to light up the world? My heart bleeds for the little ones who don't have an example to follow. We are the salt of the earth. When will we begin to show our flavor? When will we begin to season the earth with our goodness? All things work together for the good of those who love Me and are called according to My purpose; but when will you move into action to bless the lost and those in need of direction? Such a hurting, dying world. No need for this. If My people were in place, there would be a change in the atmosphere so great that the world would have to stand up and take notice. What a mighty God you serve! Your mouth is a mouthpiece for My Glory! Use it to bless not curse. Walk with a sweet savor and bless everything in your path. With the salt of My goodness, through My Word, bring healing and wholeness to the body, mind and spirit. Resist the temptation to speak what you think. Be not afraid. I will be with you always and I will accomplish what I set out to do. I will give you the peace that passes all understanding as you go about your tasks. Know that I Am with you always. Write the vision and make it plain.

Eyes have not seen, nor ears heard the things I have prepared for you, My child. I Am the Alpha and the Omega, the first and the last. I rule everything with My outstretched arms. Rest assured your secret thoughts are safe with Me. I know them and will deal with each situation to bring deliverance. All things work together for good for those who love Me and are called according to My purpose. Listen to Me and I will reveal to you mysteries; what to say, and what to do, and when. I Am the light that shines in this dark world. I have called you to be a light too. Walk in the light and shine brightly, My child.

Transition

Behold, I will do a new thing; now it shall spring forth. Trust Me, to walk with you, and talk with you, all the days of your life. I Am the Good Shepherd, and no one who follows Me, wants. You are in a place of transition. Listen closely for My voice. I will lead you to all truth. Do not be afraid of making mistakes. I will catch you if you begin to fall. Your life is in My hands. Trust Me for every good and perfect gift. I will enlighten you to see, when you need to see. Everything that glitters is not gold. Trust Me to bring about everything that I promised you. Be anxious for nothing. In due time, you shall reap a harvest. Your labor is not in vain. Continue learning from Me. I take pleasure in your pursuit of My Word. Hide it in the recesses of your heart so it shall spring up as a brook of water overflowing to share with those I send you.

Believe

I Am the Lord your God! Nothing is too hard for Me. I told you if you ask, you shall receive. Believe My promises for I am not a mere man that I should lie. Come into My presence and serve Me with your whole heart.

Many have walked before you who have been tempted and fallen in sin. You have been strong and fought the good fight. Hold on and be strong. Your help is on the way, bringing deliverance, peace and healing to every area where you hurt. I Am God, your provider, healer, deliverer, peace, and righteousness. Nothing shall I withhold from them who walk upright before Me, and have the desire to do My Will, in the earth. I want to show My Queens what it is like to have a King. Just hold on a little while longer. All I have promised is coming.

With all of the things I have done for you; you still do not believe I can do it? I will do it! Nothing is too hard for Me.

Seeing is believing, but those who have faith are mine. I love you with an everlasting love! No one can take you out of My hand. I will preserve you, nurture you, and keep you in My care forever. Your heart loves without reason. You care for those who are cast aside, unwanted or who need a friend. You are a good friend to all who befriend you, yet your heart gets hurt, time after time, by those who don't appreciate the blessing you are to them. Such a friend, who bends over backwards, to bring a smile or laugh to those in distress. Rebuke the devourer in your midst. You will know them by their fruit. I love you with an everlasting love. I shall not falter in My care for you. I Am an all-consuming fire. I will burn up anything, in your life, that is not like Me. You will come forth as pure gold!

All things are possible to the one that believes. Set your mind and your heart on my presence. Never depart. I love you and my love will never depart. Keep loving me and believing in yourself. All you need is locked up inside of you waiting to come out and bless this sin sick world. Never wonder if I am with you. I said I will never leave you nor forsake you. Trust me in all things. I will work things out for your good and My glory. Never doubt about how I will bring you out. I said, I will, and it is already done.

Discernment

You are wonderfully, awesomely made! You have discernment, and knowledge, to assist you in your decision-making process. Draw from My Word, and your innate abilities to discern what is My Will. You are growing daily in your discernment. I will not let you fall. Continue to learn on Me and judge everything by My Word. I will never leave you nor forsake you. I will be with you forever; to the end of time. I love you with an everlasting love; unconditionally. Let Me heal the hole in your heart so that you can embrace Me fully, your ultimate love, and the King I Am preparing for you.

Destiny

Be still and know that I Am God! I orchestrate situations and circumstances to be a blessing to My children. I Am able to work out every situation or circumstance of difficulty in your life. I Am! Rest in knowing I Am in control of this situation. Give Me the opportunity to work a blessing in it for you. Eyes have not seen, nor ears heard the blessings I have, for My obedient children. Walk in the fullness of My blessings for you. Do not be afraid. I Am with you always, to the end of time. Forgive those who have wronged you knowing that they know not what they have done. Have mercy on them. Walk in My Peace, Joy, Love, Kindness, Gentleness, Self-Control, Patience, and Faithfulness. I love you with an everlasting love! I will surprise you with riches. It all belongs to Me. Since your heart desires the spiritual life more than the worldly life, I have more in store for you. I Am the Lover of your soul. No man can ever satisfy you the way I can, but since you live in the flesh, I will allow one of My servants to be a major blessing in your life in the flesh. He will love you and provide for all of your earthly needs. However, he will never be able to take My place in your heart because you are sold out to Me and the plan I have for your life. He will be a support to you to complete the plan I have for you. Eyes have not seen, nor ears heard, the blessings I have in store for you, My child! I love you with an everlasting love. You are very precious to Me. One of My gems. I will not allow anyone to use or abuse you or sabotage the plans I have for you. Be still and listen for My instructions. Do not be deceived. I Am not mocked. Prepare for the things I have in store for you. Major blessings coming your way! Just wait and see how much I love you and want to bless you with the riches I have. You are the apple of My eye, daughter. I love you dearly and cherish every waking moment that you sit with Me to hear from Me. Even when I don't speak with you, the very act of you getting up and sitting in My presence blesses Me. You are blessed and highly favored. Nothing is too good for you. You deserve the best; My finest gifts. I will not spare any, nor tarry to provide them to you. Just be patient as I set My plan in motion; then enjoy the ride! Blessed be the name of the Lord! My Son died for your salvation and freedom. He died so that you would be set free from the bondage of sin, and to allow you to come directly to Me in prayer. Do not forget to be diligent in your prayer life. I love talking with you, and don't want to miss any precious moments with you. I will heal you and your land. It is a part of your inheritance. The marriage bed is not defiled. When you lie down to receive the blessings of making love, do not be concerned about whether or not I Am pleased with you. It is an act of worship unto Me. I will make it pleasing for both of you. Do not worry. I enjoy My children being pleasured in the way I ordained them to be. I oversee the intimacy and will surely make the time pleasing, exceedingly to both of you. Don't worry. It will work out for your good and My glory. I Am God! I Am your Father, and I take pleasure in every aspect of your life! Relax and rest assured, as you yield yourself to Me, I will bring these things to fruition. It pleases Me to bless you.

Your thanksgiving gives Me pleasure! A sweet incense in My nostrils! Keep the lines of communication open with Me. Stay connected to the vine. Continue to read My Word to be strengthened and for My instructions. Forsake not the small beginnings. There is much I want to share with you. Be patient and watch My hand move. I can move mountains, and I shall! Be still and know that I Am God!

You love deeply. Be careful not to be deceived by wolves in sheep's clothing. Some are ravenous wolves out to steal, kill, and destroy the plans I have for your life. Guard your heart with all diligence. I need people working in the vineyard to strengthen the family unit, My prized possessions. Family brings joy to My children's hearts. Do not be afraid of the future tasks and responsibilities. You are well equipped to handle them with My help. I have been preparing you all along, for such a time as this. I will promote you and keep you as you follow My instructions. You have done well up to this point. Continue to follow My instructions, to the letter, and you will enjoy the fruit of your labor. Don't listen to naysayers and those who I have not revealed the special blessings and assignments for your life. Grow in the peace and admonition of My Son, as I nurture you to wholeness, in Me. Remember daughter, life and death are in the power of the tongue. Speak life! Encourage at all times; be gentle in proceeding; think and pray before speaking. I will lead you every step of the way. Be strong in the Lord and the power of His might. I will do it!

(Psalm 118-4, Psalm 113:709, Psalm 91-4)

For the next five days, journal every day and I will make things clear for you. You are a sheep from My flock. I love you and want to see your progression as you follow My directions closely. I love you with an everlasting love. I will not leave you or forsake you. Look to Me for all of your needs and I will provide. With loving kindness, I will bless you. Cast all of your cares on Me. I care for you. Blessings abound! With My friendship comes joy, peace, long suffering, gentleness, kindness, love, faithfulness, goodness and self-control. You are My masterpiece broken for the birth of others; compassionate to help heal their wounds, blessed with joy to bring sunshine into their dull days. I love you; don't forget it! You are blessed to be a blessing to the nations. I've been forming your character for many years now. You are ready to pour out into the hearts of My people. I will be there with you every step of the way. Don't worry about man; he cannot harm you when I have My Almighty hand covering you.

I Am the Lord your God! Suffer not the little children; let them come to Me boldly and with reverence. I will mend those with a broken heart and a contrite spirit. (Includes babies in Christ.) You are a mouthpiece to the nations. Do not allow people to box you in to the four walls. I will deliver you and keep you. In My presence there is fullness of joy! Do not concern yourself with things. I will take care of you. You are Mine and I Am concerned with whatever concerns you. Pray without ceasing and My will, and way, will be revealed to you.

I got your back! I will never leave you nor forsake you. Trust and believe in Me. Seek My face and you will be able to do all things necessary to enjoy an abundant life. You are precious. I love you with an everlasting love. Fret not. All things work together for the good of those who love Me and are called according to My purpose. Forsake not My little ones. They are all precious in My sight. You are not alone. I have assigned angels to walk with you.

Oh, ye of little faith! Step out into the deep and bring in a haul. You are fearfully and wonderfully made. I love you with an everlasting love. Be not afraid of wrongdoers. They will not prosper in the long run. They will get their just due at the end of time. Be strong in the Lord and the power of His might. You shall reap if you faint not. I Am with you always until the end of time. I meant what I said, when I said, what I said to you. I Am not a man that I should lie. Only truth comes from My lips to your ears. Be humble in speech. I love you with and ever, loving love. You are My Ambassador. Speak what I speak, do what I say to do, touch who I say to touch and deliver what I say to deliver, with no side-stepping. This is serious work; not for the faint at heart. You are strong and able to withstand the attacks of the enemy. Be of good courage.

You are mine. I love you with an uncompromising love. Be not afraid of wrongdoers and wrongdoings. I have conquered them all. Be strong in the Lord and the power of His might. He will not let you be put to shame. You have worked for every blessing you are about to receive. All things do work together for the good of those who love the Lord and follow His precepts. I Am not mocked. You will reap what you sow. If you reap a better harvest then what you have sowed, it's because of My grace and mercy. I do not lie. I Am the one true, living God and I don't fail at anything. If I say it, it shall come to pass.

Master Plan

You are My pride and joy. There is nothing I will not do for one of My obedient children. However, timing is the issue. You must be patient and wait on My hand to move. I will move on your behalf in My right timing. Master plans take great work and proper timing. Wait on Me to bring My plan to fruition. Great plans have proper planning. You must die to your flesh at this time to reap the harvest at the appointed time. You are full of questions. You must trust Me to see the salvation of the Lord. All things work together for good for those who love Me and follow My precepts. I Am in charge and I have your best interest at heart. You are such a blessing to the Body of Christ; your smile, your loving heart, your demeanor.

Nothing Is Too Hard For God

My child, with all of the things I have done for you, you still do not believe I can do it? I will do it! Nothing is too hard for Me.

Mindset

My child, I love you with an everlasting love! No one can make Me change My mind about you.

Season

I Am the God of Now. As well as yesterday and tomorrow, but Now, right NOW. You are in your season to receive the blessings of the Lord. No more will you have to go through this test of endurance. You have been tried and tested and you have passed with flying colors. Hold on to your faith. Everything will be alright. No matter what it looks like right now, I Am in the Now! I make all things new. Be strong in the Lord and the power of His might. He will bring you out. Listen for His instructions. He will bring clarity. The earth is the Lord's and the fullness thereof. Rest in what you already know. God will never leave you nor forsake you. Rest. He has a mighty plan for your life. I'm preparing to take you on the ride of your life. Get ready!

Hope

My beloved, no eyes have seen nor ears heard what I have for those who love Me. You have forgotten your first love. Be strong in the Lord and the power of His might. I take pleasure in spending time with you. Don't despise the day of small beginnings. I work things out for your good and My Glory! Trust Me. I will never leave you nor forsake you. When I speak, you will hear and respond. You are a faithful servant. You have been off course lately. Your focus has been on man rather than on Me. If you keep your eyes focused on Me, I will take care of those things that concern you. Sometimes we focus on the wrong things and it causes us to worry unnecessarily. I Am your hope! The hope of glory! No man goes to the Father except through Me. I Am the Vine and you are one of the branches. Trust Me in all things. I will not lead you astray. Believe in My Word and it shall come to fruition.

Victorious

I, the Lord God, Am your keeper. I alone keep you from stumbling. Rest in Me, as I rest in you. I will bring "new life" within your members. Cast down vain imaginations. My Words are life and truth. In Me alone will you trust. I Am the Alpha and Omega. I knew you, and loved you, before the foundations of the world. Reverence Me with your tithes and offerings, as you did before. Do not be afraid of man. He can do you no harm. I Am with you, to cover you, and to keep you, from harm and danger. I will not send you out alone, to the wolves, ready to devour you. I will protect you with one of My mighty warriors, who has been trained and equipped to battle the forces. I Am not a man that I should lie. Look to Me with radiant joy. Out of Me flows the rivers of life. You too possess the rivers of life overflowing. Walk according to the just, not the unjust. You see yourself as downtrodden, defeated. I see you as a victorious, a winner! You have won the small victories that I have placed before you. No weapon formed against you shall prosper, and every tongue that rises in judgement, shall be cut down. I Am God your deliverer, healer, helper, and lawyer in the courtroom. You are victorious! With Me, you have it all! Believe and trust that what you hear from Me is true. I Am not a man that I should lie. Don't try so hard to make things happen. You are not the deliverer. I Am, that I Am. Take My yolk upon you. My yolk is easy, and My burden is light. Learn from Me, and you shall live in the midst of this wicked world. My Words are truth and life to the believer. Believe and live. Walk humbly in My presence and serve Me. Don't worry about what people say. They are not your redeemer or deliverer. I love you with and everlasting love. I trust you to walk the walk, and talk the talk I have given you, in My Word. You are My friend. I love you so much. Every hurt or pain you have experienced, has been to help others grow in their walk with Me. Do not be afraid. I shield you from all harm and danger as you are led by My Holy Spirit. I will not lead you to destruction, rather abundant life in Me, your Redeemer. Follow Me and be of good courage. You will have friends and enemies; all for My purposes to be fulfilled. I don't expect you to understand right now. But you will get understanding as we continue this journey. I will deliver without delay Trust Me. (Psalm 118) Peace. Be still, quiet, and learn.

When I Am for you, who can be against you? I Am the Bread of Life, eat and be filled! For I know the plans I have for you. Plans for your good, and hope for the future. Do not allow the enemy to taint the truth I have placed in you. I Am a jealous God, and I will not allow any idols before Me. Put your life in order with Me first. I Am the Hope of Glory! I Am the answer to all of your problems and questions. I hold the key to every dream or desire you have. I pick up where you end. When you come to the end of yourself, I will be there, in all My Glory, with arms outstretched, waiting for you. I desire to wrap My arms around you and fill you with the peace that passes understanding, and the love that loves past feelings, and pain. A love that never ends.

Inseparable

I Am the Lord your God. You shall have no false gods before Me. Pick up your cross and follow Me. Though the road may be rough and the going tough, I Am with you always. You are My precious one. I will not delay in performing My work in you and through you. Stand strong with your loins gird with the gospel of truth. I will never depart from your presence. Keep Me in the center of your will and plan for your life. Though you are afraid, you will not stumble. I Am with you, to strengthen you, and keep you from falling into diverse temptations. Lean on Me, and I will keep you from falling. Strengthened by My Word, you will prophesy until the rocks cry out for My presence. You have been listening to too many voices of concern. Listen for My voice only. I will not deceive you nor lead you astray. I Am not a man; I do not lie. Come to Me all who are heavy laden, and I will give you rest. These words are a comfort to all who are weary in well doing. I know what it's like to be taken for granted. The ten lepers were healed, and only one came back to thank Me; countless other examples are in My Word. Focus on Me, and you will find rest, and direction, even in the midst of difficulty and raging storms. I love you with an ever-loving love. You will never experience the love I have for you through a human being; only with Me. I made you that way, so that no one can take My place in your life. Count it all joy, when you go through many temptations. All is well! Life is designed to challenge you, in things that will allow you to show forth My Glory! I love you with an everlasting love. I won't take you through anything that is not necessary to show forth My Glory. You are Mine. Don't forget, you are Mine. I know what is best for your life, and I will see it to completion. Your life will shine forth My Glory; on earth, and above the earth, from everlasting to everlasting. You are a gem; a diamond in the rough. Step out into the deep, so that you can bring in a haul of souls for harvest. Wrap your loving arms around My children to give them comfort, in the time of trouble. I will always be with you. Your arms are My arms; your words of comfort are My words. Be not dismayed. God is not mocked. What man meant for evil, shall be for your good. I love you and will always love you; even when you don't feel My presence. All things do work together for the good of those who love Me and are called according to My purpose. You are called. Follow Me in word, and deed, to the ends of the earth. You will always find Me, when you seek Me with all of your heart. Sunrise and sunset; praise Me. I'm worthy! I died, so that you might have life, and have it more abundantly; not things, but life. I Am the one true, loving God, who has no limits; no boundaries. Tap into My waters that flow to overflowing. In My presence is fullness of joy! Keep encouraging yourself through My Word. Praise and worship are My delights. I love fellowshipping with you, and long for each and every moment I spend with you. You are special to Me. Never forget how much I love you. You are My peach, and the apple of My eye! Nothing can separate you from My love. Nothing can separate us!

Light

Sit in quiet communion with Me. I Am the Alpha and Omega; first and last. No one is greater. Follow My precepts to have everlasting life. Stay connected to the vine of the tree of life. All things work together for good. In Me you will find no darkness; only light. Do not be deceived by those imitating light. The enemy comes as an angel of light, but you will know My children, by the goodness of the fruit they bring to the table. Good fruit does not spoil quickly. Speak My truths, in love, to draw sinners to repentance. I love you with an everlasting love. I will not leave or forsake you.

I Am the Alpha and the Omega, the first and the last. Jesus is the light of the world. There is no darkness in Him. I love you with an everlasting love. Eyes have not seen, nor ears heard the things I have prepared for you. Keep your light shining bright. No matter what happens, keep your light shining bright. I will never leave you, nor forsake you. For I Am that light of the world!

I Am the vine, you are the branches, live in Me and abide in Me and your life will be complete. I love you with an ever-loving love. No one can take My place in your life. I'm jealous when you allow others to take up residence in your heart, mind and spirit, more than Me. I Am your light. I will light and lead your way. Eyes have not seen, nor ears heard, the things I have prepared for you. Do not be afraid. I Am always with you. I provide peace continually. Do not worry about your future. I've got it covered. Your bread is to believe in Me. I will bring it to fruition.

I Am the light and your salvation. None other is greater than Me. Walk in the light of My Presence. I will not leave you alone. Do not be afraid of man. He cannot hurt you. You are mine. You belong to Me. The cares of this world are not yours. Leave them to Me. Kiss them goodbye. Follow Me, and you never have to worry about being led astray. I Am the Alpha and Omega. Worship Me in Spirit and in truth. I will never lead you astray. Cling to My Word as your Sword and Shield; a buckler in the time of trouble. I will never leave you or forsake you. You are not alone. So many things vie for your attention, but keep your focus on Me, the solid rock on which you stand; everything else is sinking sand.

Eyes have not seen, nor ears heard the things I have prepared for you, My child. I Am the Alpha and the Omega, the first and the last. I rule everything with My outstretched arms. Rest assured your secret thoughts are safe with Me. I know them and will deal with each situation to bring deliverance. All things work together for good for those who love Me and are called according to My purpose. Listen to Me and I will reveal to you mysteries; what to say, and what to do, and when. I Am the light that shines in this dark world. I have called you to be a light too. Walk in the light and shine brightly, My child.

Battles

For we walk by faith and not by sight! I Am the Lord your God. Never have I seen the righteous forsaken or their seed begging for bread. All things work together for the good of those who love the Lord and are called according to My purpose. No weapon formed against you shall prosper, and every tongue that speaks against you shall be cut down. Humble yourself before the mighty hand of God, and in due season you shall prosper and eat off of the fat of the land. Walk in My presence and serve Me. I Am the vine and you are one of the branches. Stay connected to Me, and you will live, and love again. Take your time with Me. I Am a patient God, willing to work with you, through all adversity, pleasure and pain. Keep your eyes focused on Me, the God of your salvation. I can do all things but fail. I see you crying. I see all of your tears and know all of your fears. I will not push you off of a cliff and expect you to fly. I'll never leave you nor forsake you, for I Am your God, mighty in power. I never fail! Be still and know that I Am God! I will be exalted above the heavens, and the earth! Do not be afraid! I Am not mocked. Truth is truth, and it will never be a lie. Stand.

Having done all you can do, stand. Let Me fight your battles. I'm fully capable of working it out for your good and My glory.

Focus

I Am the light and your salvation. None other is greater than Me. Walk in the light of My Presence. I will not leave you alone. Do not be afraid of man. He cannot hurt you. You are mine. You belong to Me. The cares of this world are not yours. Leave them to Me. Kiss them goodbye. Follow Me, and you never have to worry about being led astray. I Am the Alpha and Omega. Worship Me in Spirit and in truth. I will never lead you astray. Cling to My Word as your Sword and Shield; a buckler in the time of trouble. I will never leave you or forsake you. You are not alone. So many things vie for your attention, but keep your focus on Me, the solid rock on which you stand; everything else is sinking sand.

Sow To The Spirit

I Am the Lord your God. You shall have no false gods before Me. The flowers in the field grow and take no care for how they thrive; do so likewise. I Am the Lord your God, and I Am your provider; glean from Me. Sow not to the flesh, or you shall reap the things of the flesh. Sow to the Spirit and receive the bountiful blessings that overflow from the Spirit! Pray in the Spirit at all times. Manifested blessings will flow through you and great works shall come to fruition.

Security

I Am the Lord your God, happy is he that resides in Me! You are a product of your environment. This is why a man must leave his house and cleave to his wife. Change, sometimes, only comes about, when you get out of your familiar environment and into the land flowing with milk and honey. Be not afraid. I Am with you. My rod and My staff give you courage. Be not afraid of naysayers. I Am God! Alpha and Omega; first and last! No evil shall come upon you, or your family, as you stay hidden under My wings. Praise the wonderful name of Jesus! Do not worry about what you are to eat or what you are to wear. I have taken care of your provisions. Trust Me. I Am not a man that I should lie. I Am Love and Truth.

Passion

I love you with an everlasting love! You're a bouquet of roses, red in color! Red is for passion! I'm passionately in love with you! I need you to be passionately in love with yourself. The passionate one lives inside of you! You are not forsaken. I'm passionately in love with you! I cherish every tear you cry, even when you think you are crying in an ugly way, I love you! Relax in My presence where you can experience the fullness of joy! Hear My voice and obey My every command. You will eat from the good of the land. I love you with an everlasting love. I want what is best for you. I have your best interest at heart. I will never leave nor forsake you. I Am your God, and you are My lamb. Not many days from now, you will see a manifestation of My glory. Be not afraid. I love you and want what is best for you. Be ready for the manifestation. It's for the appointed time.

Release

I Am the Lord your God! You are a precious soul trying to control your every move. I Am the God who is your source and salvation! I will save you from anything that tries to come against My will for your life. Be not afraid. I Am with you. Embrace My presence daily. I love you with an everlasting love. You will not be put to shame. Those who try to shame you, will themselves be put to shame. Guard your heart with My Word. I have a love for you that is deeper than the ocean. Listen to My Words of instruction. Let go of those things which are behind and press towards the mark of the high calling of Jesus.

It Shall Come To Past!

Be thou not dismayed, for as surely as the sun is in the sky, and the stars at night, so will My Word be accomplished. It shall not return void, but it shall accomplish all it set forth to accomplish. It shall come to past! Wait on it. I know what's best for you. I will make you prosperous and to have good success!

I Am the Lord your God. Listen to Me. Famines will arise in the land. Store up the goods for healthy eating and living. Family is an integral part of life. Cherish time and moments for joy. It will all come to past as I have said. Rejoice in the Lord and do good for the Kingdom of God is at hand. I'm doing a new thing. Don't you perceive it? Listen to Me, and I will give you the secrets to life. Hold fast to My unchanging hand. I will not let you stumble into sin. You are precious in My sight. I love you with an everlasting love. Do not tremble or faint at the things I ask you to do. I Am God and all things are possible with Me. If I ask you to do it, I will see you through it. For nothing is impossible with Me. I love you with a never-ending love. Trust Me to bring all the things I spoke to you to past.

❖

All things are possible to the one that believes. Set your mind and your heart on my presence. Never depart. I love you. My love will never depart. Keep loving me and believing in yourself. All you need is locked up inside of you waiting to come out and bless this sin sick world. Never wonder if I am with you. I said, I will never leave you nor forsake you. Trust me in all things. I will work things out for your good and My glory. Never doubt about how I will bring you out. I said, I will, and it is already done.

❖

I love you with and everlasting love. There is nothing too hard for Me. Be patient with My plans. They shall come to past in due season. I will unfold as you sit back and watch. Let not your heart be troubled, believe in Me and I will work all things out for your good and My glory. Be not afraid. I Am with you through it all. Do not fear these divers of trials, all have come to make you stronger; to build character.

I Am the Alpha and Omega, first and last. All things are possible with Me. Be not afraid. I Am with you. My rod and My staff give you courage. Lean on My never changing hand. I love you with an everlasting love. No one can compare, with the love I have for you. Be ye ever ready to do whatever I ask you to do. This is the law and the prophets; that you love one another, as I have loved you; from everlasting to everlasting. I will never withdraw My love for you. Like a tree planted by the water My love, you shall not be moved. Whatever I have told you, I shall bring it to past. Wait on Me to tell you when to move. My timing is impeccable. It is always right.

Deliverance & Healing

I Am the God of ancient days. I Am the God of the past, present and future. I have already planned a good life for you. Walk in it and be prosperous. You're trying to use your mind to figure it out, instead of using your heart to walk it out. I Am the God of Love everlasting. Fear no one. I Am in charge of all. I Am the creator and the lifter of your soul! Listen to Me and be saved, set free, and delivered from the opinions of man. I was silent during your time of need to test you and see if you would implement what I had been telling you to do. Your disobedience can cause you to miss out on the very things that I plan to bless you with. Be steadfast and unmovable, always abiding in My Word. Be not afraid. Whatever a man soweth, that also shall he reap. May the peace that passes all understanding rule and abide, to keep you from falling into the traps, plots and the snares of the enemy. Know your worth. Mend broken hearts with My Word and My love. I will bless you and keep you. Be not afraid of fiery trials. They will come but I Am with you always, never to depart.

Heartbreak

Put on the whole armor of God. Exciting things are coming to past! Be still and enjoy My Presence. You are the apple of My eye, the lily of the valley, the bright and shining star! I love you with a never-ending love. Do not forget My sacrifice for you. Hold tight to My never changing hand and I will deliver. I love you and have seen your heartbreak. Know that I Am with you always. When you suffer, I suffer alongside you, but you must go through the tests, to bless others with the testimonies of how you made it through. Stand strong and remember, I Am with you always until the end of time. You will survive! You're not happy with the twists and turns in your life but trust Me, there is great purpose being birthed. I love you with a never-ending love. I know what is best for you. I've got your back, always. Do not fear, only believe, trust and obey.

Immobilize

Quiet and still your mind so you can grasp hold of the wonderful things I have planned for you. You are the salt of the earth. Bring your mind under submission to the things I have spoken to you. Write the vision and make it plain. Eyes have not seen, and ears have not heard, the things I have prepared for you! Widen your tent. You will receive from the north, south, east and west. It is My plan for your life that you are prosperous and have good success. Fret not. You have nothing to be afraid of. I Am with you. My rod and My staff give you courage. Peace I give to you. A mere man can do nothing to harm you. You are in My care and I Am a good Shepherd. I protect, lead, guide and direct. Straighten this house up. It will help you to feel better about yourself and your accomplishments. It's time to take off the sackcloth and immobilize. You are not a wounded warrior. You are mighty in battle to the tearing down of strongholds. Do not be deceived. God is not mocked. Sowers will reap their harvest according to what seeds were sowed.

Bedroom Sanctuary

Your bedroom should be your sanctuary. Only the things that bring glory to God should be in there to help you to enjoy the beauty of holiness in your sanctuary. It should be kept clean and fresh. The colors should be restful, peaceful, and exotic, to show adventure and peace can coincide together. Soft fragrances and soft music for meditation or relaxation. Make it inviting, comfortable, calming, clean, soft and enjoyable. Sit in My presence and serve Me with gladness and joy! Give Me all the glory and honor. Worship Me in the beauty of holiness, without which no one will see Me.

Covering

Fear not! The Lord is with thee bringing good tidings! Blessed are they that strive for righteousness, peace, love and joy. Peacemakers, in the Kingdom of God, shall see God. Fret not over things or people that have no heaven or hell to put you in. Delight in Me and I will give you the desires of your heart! Believe and receive the blessings and benefits I bestow on you and your family. Things aren't always as they seem. Hearts are hidden to protect the innocent. Evil doers will be punished in the end. Whatever you sow that also shall you reap. Sow wisely. Use keen discernment in your interactions with others, My masterpiece, broken for the birth of others, compassionate to help heal their wounds, blessed with joy to bring sunshine into their dull days. I love you. Don't forget it. I've been forming your character for many years now. You are ready to pour out into the hearts of My people. I will be there with you every step of the way. Don't worry about man; he cannot harm you when I have My Almighty hand covering you.

Procrastination

Greater is He in you, than he in this world. Greater is coming! Be aware. Stay awake. Do not slumber or sleep on the things I have instructed you to do. Timing is a factor. Challenges help your brain to grow with strategies and ideas.

Overcomer

Do not fear. You have been called for such a time as this. I will lead, guide and direct you in the ways that you shall go. My right hand is upon you to keep you from hurt, harm and danger. You are an overcomer! With Me, all things are possible!

Attacks

Hold fast to what I have taught you. Do not be swayed by popular opinion, clothes, money, or cars. These things are fleeting. Victory comes from being steadfast, unmovable and always abiding in My Word. You are a sheep from My flock. Listen to those whom I assign you to for instruction. They will not lead you astray. Be consistent in loving and giving. Time is short. Be prepared with the Sword of the Spirit to combat the attacks of the enemy. Keep on the full armor of God. You never know the day nor the hour of attack; however, I will notify you, so you may prepare further, but be ready.

You are mine. I love you with an uncompromising love. Be not afraid of wrongdoers and wrongdoings. I have conquered them all. Be strong in the Lord and the power of His might. I will not let you be put to shame. You have worked for every blessing you are about to receive. All things do work together for the good of those who love the Lord and follow His precepts. I Am not mocked. You will reap what you sow. If you reap a better harvest then what you have sowed, it's because of My grace and mercy. I do not lie. I Am the one true, living God and I don't fail at anything. If I say it, it shall come to fruition.

Victory

I Am the Lord your God. Behold I bring you glad tidings! The Joy of the Lord is your strength! Do not allow anyone to steal your joy. Walk upright before Me at all times. I know you are flesh, and unable to walk this walk perfectly without Me. Lean on Me, and lean not to your own understanding, but rely and trust what I tell you, and act on it. I love you unconditionally. I will not leave you or forsake you. I know you love Me, and have a heart, to do things the way I instruct you to do. I know what you are going to say, before you say it, and I know your thoughts and actions, before you think or act. I will be with you to lead, guide and direct. Wait on My instructions. You know My voice, and a stranger you will not follow. You are Mine. I love you with an everlasting love. I know you, and I still love you. You are Mine. Be strong in the Lord and the power of His might. You will not lose. You have the victory in Christ Jesus! Don't concern yourself with what others say, or do, about you. My right hand covers you.

Relax

Keep your eyes focused on Me. I will lead, guide and direct you into all of the right opportunities and doors, that will be a great blessing, and opportunity for you. Relax. I am in charge and I love you. I know what is best, and I will lead you to whatever is best for you. Hold on. Help is on the way. You are not alone. I'm your buckler and shield. I see all, know all, and grieve all. Joy comes in the morning! It's your time and your season for miraculous blessings!

Strategy

Strategic planning is My expertise! I strategically placed the stars in the sky and caused everything to work together for My Glory! Stop allowing things around you to distract you. Do not be afraid. I Am with you. Don't look to the east or west, north or south. Keep your eyes focused on Me and I will give you the desires of your heart. Be not afraid of the noisy pestilence that flies by day. Enlarge your tent. Your blessings will outnumber the stars in the sky. Your reward in heaven will be great! Lean on Me, the Master of your will. I will make it happen.

Practicing His Presence

All that glitters, is not gold. Use wisdom in all of your doings. My hand is upon you leading, guiding and directing you to an expected end. Do not fear! I love you with unconditional love. My Spirit I have placed in you to lead, guide, direct and protect you from hurt, harm and danger. Trust Me to do what I said I would do. Grow in the grace and admonition of the Father in heaven. Practice His presence. In His presence there is joy, peace, protection, direction and everlasting life. All you need is in His presence. Practice His presence. Be still to hear the still, small voice that assures you of My presence. In My presence, is fullness of joy. Be not afraid! Anything that I ask you to do will be under my watchful eyes and capable hands. I will not leave you nor forsake you. I Am your Savior, Redeemer and Lord of your life. It is My job to be with you and lead you to righteousness, peace, love, and joy. Trust Me and I will do it!

Bask in My presence, you who feel so misunderstood. In My presence is fullness of joy! All of what you need to sustain you, is in My presence.

Be Not Weary

Arise, O highly favored of the Lord! Be not weary in well doing, for you shall reap a harvest if you faint not.

My precious, inquisitive child; all things work together for the good of those who love Me and are called according to My purposes. Be not weary in well-doing. You shall reap a harvest if you faint not. The time is coming, and is not far off, when you will want a time of rest. All of what you are doing is under My watchful eyes. Sin not. Be attentive. Your enemies desire to sift you like wheat. Hold on to the blood, stained banner. Hold on to My word, planted deep in your heart. Realize you are flesh, and unable to be victorious without My help. I will never leave you, nor forsake you. You can count on Me. Dry your eyes. Weeping may endure for a night, but joy comes in the morning. It's morning!

Be Still

Be still and know that I Am God. Worship and adore Me. Praise Me in the sanctuary. Lessons learned are precious in My sight. I know every bump and bruise. I know your frustrations when you lay down and get up. Leave them all with Me, the guardian of your soul. Fear not, because I Am with you always, until the end of time. You are Mine and I love you with an everlasting love. Be steadfast and unmovable, always abiding in My love for you. Be of good cheer because I have conquered everything that troubles you. I Am God and nothing is too hard for Me. Everything is possible with Me. I will lead and guide you to all truth. Trust Me.

I Am the Lord your God; there are none like Me! Relax and know that I Am God. I created the heavens with My right hand. Is anything too hard for Me? Listen carefully for My voice. I will lead, guide and direct you to all truth. Anything not truth, is not Me. You are the head, and not the tail; the lender, and not the borrower. All power is in

My hand. Trust Me. I love you with an everlasting love. Be still and know that I Am Almighty God.

❖

You are My precious jewel. All things work together for the good of those who love Me and are called according to My purposes. Be still and know that I Am God. I work all things for your good, and My glory. This situation is a temporary setback, in preparation for the setup I have for you. Be patient, and learn from Me. I have not forsaken you. Trust Me, and you will see My hand at work. It is well.

❖

For you were bought with a price. Be still and know that I Am God. Do not be afraid. What can man do to you when I Am your God?

Follow The Directions

Do not be dismayed. I Am with you to lead you to all that is seen and unseen. I Am God! There is none other. Glorify Me with your life. Take time to smell the roses, then you will hear clearly from Me. Once you did things your own way. Now you will follow My directions and I will lead you to what eyes have not seen, and ears have not heard. I've shown you some things from the supernatural, but there is much more! Trust Me to lead, guide and direct your steps. I will not let you fall. Grip My never changing hand. All things do work together for the good of those who love Me and are called according to my purposes. Man forsakes you, but I never will.

Trust & Obey

I Am the Lord your God. You shall have no other gods before Me. When I say go, you go. When I say stay, you stay. I will lead you and guide you by day and by night. Your ancestors followed the cloud by day and the moon by night. I speak directly to you and expect you to respond according to what I have told you to do. Do not be afraid when what I tell you to do seems strange. Just as Jesus used mud from His spit to open the blind man's eyes and told the ten lepers to wash in the dirty waters to be healed. My ways are not your ways, and My thoughts are higher than your thoughts. Don't question My methods, just trust Me to heal and deliver. My sheep hear My voice and will not follow another. Listen closely for My voice. Do not be deceived. Follow what I tell you, and use My Word as your reference guide, to know My will, and My ways. I will not lead you astray. You are My precious daughter whom I love dearly. Stay close to Me and I will see to it you make it to your destiny with joy. The joy of the Lord is your strength. Stay sure-footed in the faith and grow in the love and admonition of the Lord your God and Savior. He never leaves you nor forsakes you. He is with you always.

Hold on to His never changing hand. He will not lead you astray. Stay close to Him and you will be safe from hurt, harm and danger. The lusts of this world seek to devour the good in you. You are good and embody the love of the Lord in your heart, mind and spirit. Just trust Me to do what only I can do. I'm in the miracle making business, and I love blessing people with things that grow faith in Me. Sometimes things seem harsh, but there is an ultimate plan, and course, that will exhibit to the fullest, and greatest extent, My divine capabilities. They are designed to show the world, My Lordship, and to grow My family. I love you with an everlasting love. Trust and obey, and I will bring the things I promised to fruition. I will never leave you, nor forsake you. You are Mine, My beloved Queen. No matter what you have done, you have been forgiven. I don't remember the things you've done, and neither should you. Walk sure-footed in the things I've called you to do, and I will work with you, to bring the works of your hands, to fruition. Eyes have not seen, and ears have not heard, the plans I have for you; just waiting for you to line up with My desires, for your greatness in Christ. Be as wise as an owl and as cunning as a fox. You will see with your eyes, and feel with your hands, the blessings waiting to engulf you in love. I Am the Lord your God, and I do not fail.

Encouragement

Labor not in the things that are seen, but sow into the things that are unseen. Bless those who curse you with utter obscenities, injustice and lies to stop or block your progress. I Am still in charge. My Will has dominion over all the earth; things above & below. Be steadfast, unmovable, always abounding in My love. You are a beacon of light shining in massive darkness. The battle is not yours. It belongs to the Lord of hosts. I know you feel weary in well doing, but faint not. Hold on to My never changing hand and I will pull you through. I Am not a man that I should lie. Men will reap what they sow, especially if it is done with malice in their heart. I judge the heart. My grace and mercy is fresh and new every morning. It's the dawning of a new day. Recognize your faults and learn from them. I love you with an everlasting love. No matter what you do, as long as you are repentant at heart, you are forgiven. Learn to forgive completely as I forgive you. Wisdom will encompass you, and keep you from the silly mistakes you made, before maturity. Don't allow yourself to go backwards and reap the consequences of your actions before you matured. Walk in your maturity. You are fearfully and wonderfully made. I created you and I know everything about you. Come to Me and ask about anything. Be patient as you wait in expectation for your answers. I will provide. Trust My way. It will never falter. Be strong in the Lord and the power of His might. These are My words of encouragement to My people. I promise to never leave them comfortless. My words are a strong tower for the righteous to run in and be safe. There is major safety in obeying My Word. Love it, breathe it, live it, speak it, and let your actions display it. Your life is not your own. You were bought with a price. Love Me, and trust Me, to bring to pass all I have spoken to you. I will do it!

Safety

My child, fear not evil doers. They shall reap what they sow in the end. Be strong in the Lord and the power of His might. He is your best friend. He sticks closer than a brother. He loves you with an everlasting love. He will not allow you to be put to shame. Do not believe the lies of the enemy. He comes to steal and destroy the magnificent future I have planned for you. You will have joy, peace, love and contentment. Be not weary in well doing. You will reap a harvest at the set time I have chosen to bless you. Meditate on My word day and night. Know that all things work together for the good of those who love Me and follow My commands. Be of good cheer for I have conquered the world. Follow Me, and I will give you rest. You will run and not be weary or faint. I Am your strong tower. The righteous run in and are safe. Safety is found under My wings, under My watchful eye. You shall not falter. Greater is He who is in you. You shall not pass this way again. Grab hold to My goodness and favor. Do not trust the lies of man. Trust in My truths that will keep you from falling. Do not be afraid. I Am with you always. It is your time and your season. I Am holding your hand. Get up from this place and move forward into the destiny I have pre-planned to bring Me glory. Be gentle and kind. Let My love exude from you. Show My love to the masses. Restoration is here. Peace is here; joy is here; love is here. Be grateful and honor Me with thanksgiving.

Faithfulness

Great is thy faithfulness to God your Father. There is no shadow of turning away. All you have needed My hand has provided. Great is thy faithfulness, unto thee. We work well in concert with each other. I lead and you follow. You are obedient, and you seek to please Me, with your whole heart. Woe to those who try to keep you from My best in life. My arms are outstretched to give you the hug you long for, beloved. I love you with an everlasting love. Stay true to Me. I will not falter. I love you more than you can conceive. All things work together for the good of those who love Me and are called according to My purposes. Continue to be the light in the darkness. Do not dummy down to people who don't know what I have put in you. Stay true to Me as I lead, guide and direct you. Be not afraid. I Am always with you. Be strong and of good courage; I have conquered the world and everything in it. Be full of the joy of the Lord, which is your strength. Shalom, My love!

Peace

Peace be still, my love. You are blessed of the Lord and highly favored. All make mistakes: that is how you learn and grow. I made you a little lower than the angels. Be watchful.

My child, rest assured I Am with you always. I will keep you in perfect peace, if you keep your eyes on Me. You can trust Me, and I will do it.

For we walk by faith and not by sight. I gave you purpose and fashioned you when I knit you in your Mother's womb. We all desire someone to love us with a love so deep and sure. You find that love in Me. Man's love is fickle. He can't promise you the love that only I can give. I will supply all of your needs just as I promised long ago. Peace be with you always. Never worry. Never doubt. I will always bring you out.

Set your mind and your heart on my presence. I love you. My love will never depart. Keep loving me and believing in yourself. All you need is locked up inside of you, waiting to come out, and bless this sin sick world. Never wonder if I am with you. I said, I will never leave you, nor forsake you. Trust me in all things. I will work things out for your good and My glory. Never doubt about how I will bring you out. I said, I will, and it is already done.

Faith

Faith is your mantra. You will walk by faith and not by sight. I have cleared a path for you to go that will bring Me glory. Be not afraid of evil doers. They shall reap what they sow. Eyes have not seen, and ears have not heard, the wondrous things I have in store for you! You are My beloved daughter, in whom I trust. You will not fail Me in this mission of love. Stay strong and of good courage. You shall reap, if you faint not. Put on the full armor of God daily, to stand against the wiles of the devil, who roams around seeking whom he can destroy. He will not be able to destroy you. I have My hand on you and have not given him permission to harm you or your family. He can only do what I give him permission to do. I Am in charge, and I will not fail you, My love.

Be steadfast and unmovable, always abiding in the work of the Lord. Do not fear. Nothing can come against you that I cannot destroy or dismantle. Keep the faith.

Trust and never doubt. I will bring you out. Trials come to make you stronger, building up your inner man, for battles will surely come. Be strong in the Lord and the power of His might. He is the ultimate healer, mind-regulator, and provider who loves you and has sacrificed His life for you. Put on the full armor of God daily and fight the good fight of faith. Nothing shall overcome you. You are victorious in Jesus the Christ. All things work together for the good of those who love the Lord and are called according to His purpose. Always wait on the Lord for His clarity in a matter. He has the answer and He will deliver you. Be strong and of good courage. I have conquered everything you experience and so will you. Shalom.

About The Author

Ms. Tilghman is an educator, orator, author, certified life coach and mentor who earned a bachelor's degree in Liberal Studies/Specialization Communications from the American University in Washington, D.C. In 2014, after 35 years of service in the federal government, she retired from the Federal Reserve Board to focus more on her passion for teaching.

An educator at heart, over the years, Ms. Tilghman has worked with several church ministries and community projects focused on educating adults and children. Her desire after she retired was to work in the school system to encourage and impact the lives of children through teaching. She has been teaching children in the classroom for the past five years and for the past two years she has tutored students in Reading, English & Language Arts and Math during the summer months.

Ms. Tilghman is an author who has had her work published in several mediums to include an oral presentation "Life When You Are Deaf: Do You Hear What I Hear?" in 2002; a poem titled, "Patiently Waiting" published by Michele Jackson in August 2009 in the Real Life Faith Christian magazine; and a self-published children's book, "The Bubble Within" in 2014. She is currently working on a couple of other children book projects for future publication.

In addition to being an author, she is a well-versed orator who served not only as a member but also held numerous positions of leadership for Toastmasters International, Inc. for 24 years.

She is the mother of four notably, successful adult children and Nana to five amazing grandchildren.

Contact

info@scholarsexcellente.com

https://scholarsexcellente.com/